For Diane —
you are filled with
light — Shine on!
love,
Jane
6/96

WISE WOMEN DON'T WORRY, WISE WOMEN DON'T SING THE BLUES

by

Jane Claypool

For further information:
Cornucopia Press
P.O. Box 230638
Encinitas, California 92023
(619) 942-1628

Printed in the United States of America
First Printing: November 1994
Second Printing: June 1995
Third Printing: March 1996
ISBN: 0-9643948-1-2

Typography by Carol Jensen

This book is dedicated to the many wonderful women who have taught me that strength, wisdom and love are synonymous.

In particular, I thank Lucille Binder, Carol Carnes, Heather Clark, Martha Dawson, Kate DuVivier, Joan Egea, Marilyn Hall-Day, Jacquelyn Harrold, Marion Hoch, Sandy Jacob, Gina Ogden, and Anne Seislove. You are part of my Wisdom Group. You have guided me and supported me along the way. I thank you very much.

I am that supreme and fiery force that sends forth all living sparks. Death hath no part in me, yet I bestow death, wherefore I am girt about with wisdom as with wings. I am that living and fiery essence of the divine substance that glows in the beauty of the fields, and in the shining water, and in the burning sun and the moon and the stars, and in the force of the invisible winds, the breath of all living things. I breathe in the green grass and in the flowers, and in the living waters...All these live and do not die because I am in them...I am the source of the thundered word by which all creatures were made, I permeate all things that they may not die. I am life.

Abbess Hildegarde of Bingen, 1147 A.D.

TABLE OF CONTENTS

Author's Note   i

1   Wise Women Step Out   1

2   Wise Women Write Their Own Scripts   13

3   Wise Women Are Creative   19

4   Wise Women Seek Success   29

5   Wise Women Are Willing To Risk   39

6   Wise Women Know There Is A
Power For Good Working In
Their Lives   47

7   Wise Women Are Really Beautiful   55

8   Wise Women Don't Worry   65

9   Wise Women Choose Mentors   73

10   Wise Women Know How To Get Help   83

11   Wise Women Become Themselves   89

12 Wise Women Recognize Windows   97

13 Wise Women Are Assertive   103

14 Wise Women Can Change Their Minds   109

15 Wise Women Are Serene   117

16 Wise Women Know Glass
    Ceilings Are Plastic   123

17 Wise Women Can Touch Source   129

18 Wise Women Watch Their Lighting   139

19 Wise Women Are Prosperous   147

20 Wise Women Are Persistent   153

21 Wise Women Are Direct   159

22 Wise Women Don't Bear Guilt   169

23 Wise Women Believe Life Is Super
    and Natural   175

24 Wise Women Speak For Themselves   181

25 Wise Women Love Pleasure   195

26 Wise Women Let Go of The Past   205

27 Wise Women Come In All Ages   211

28 Wise Women Come In All Sizes   219

29 Wise Women Are In Process   231

30 Affirmative Prayer   239

Wise Woman Credo   253

Basic Metaphysical Ideas   254

Suggested Bibliography For Further Reading   256

About The Author   260

For Further Study   263

For More Information   264

AUTHOR'S NOTE

As we enter the second printing of *Wise Women Don't Worry, Wise Women Don't Sing the Blues*, I am pleased and somewhat startled at how quickly it is all happening. Less than six months ago, I was anxiously awaiting the first edition and hoping that the book would be well received. I'm grateful to say the book was very, very well received and is on its way to becoming a big hit!

The most difficult part of writing this book was finding a structure which would work. I wanted to use portions of my own story because the whole point of the book is that authentic power and self-reliance must come from within. It seemed to me that the book would only be authentic if I included myself. There are enough books written by "experts" who find it easy to tell others what to do but share nothing of their own selves.

I genuinely believed I was an expert on self-reliance and on personal power, not because of my studies, but because of how I'd used my studies to meet obstacles. I also believed that sharing my own faith, hope and experience was important - that at the most basic level, it was all I knew. At the same time, I wanted to demonstrate the distance from old emotional turmoil which I have achieved and which is possible for anyone.

How could I tell how it was for me and offer the suggestions, observations and wisdom I'd gained at the same time? In other words, how could I bring in the past and stay in the present? Once I figured out how I could handle my stories as stories I found the book extremely easy to write. Women tell me it is also very, very easy to read.

In just a few short months, we've sold the first printing by word of mouth. The books went to women I met in churches and to women who received them as gifts from friends. One woman purchased twenty-five books for her friends and mailed them all over the nation. Another woman has just purchased her sixth copy of the book because she keeps loaning her copy to friends who want to keep it.

Wise Women Don't Worry, Wise Women Don't Sing the Blues seems to speak to women of all ages. One woman in her early twenties told me she thought it was "great the way you used history to develop your points." I thanked her and only later did I realize that I was the history she was talking about. So if I'm history, and it helps the issues young women are facing become history, that's great!

As I write this, we are preparing the second printing. We've eliminated some typos and added this forward. The book is now being placed with distributors and in more and more bookstores. I am speaking from coast to coast and we have several Wise Women conferences and training weekends in place. The Wise Women network is forming into a national network of Wise Women groups, led by ordinary women facing ordinary issues. The book is also being used in colleges and the workplace. More ideas are in the planning stage.

The response has been marvelously gratifying. I get letters from people who say the book has changed their lives. I get visitors to the church who just read the book and want to meet me. I had one very touching encounter with a woman who swore the book saved her life. She said she was brokenhearted and considering suicide when someone offered the book to her and she decided to hang in there and go for some counseling from her minister.

Ministers become ministers because they want to help people, and I am excited about the potential I see in the Wise Women movement. Books do change lives and this book can change things for many of us.

Consider the possibilities. . .

1. Suppose everyone who reads the book and is touched by its message makes it a point to tell ten other women about the ideas she found.
2. Suppose women choose to give the book as a gift to a friend who needs it.
3. Suppose the book outreach increases exponentially, moving from thousands to tens of thousands to hundreds of thousands of readers.
4. Suppose the book finds its way into the hands of a million or more women.
5. Suppose lives are genuinely changed by the ideas in the book.

How might our world change? I love to meditate upon the possible consequences.

1. What if a million or two women decided they deserved the best?
2. What if a million or two women decided they couldn't live as victims and were going to take charge of their lives?
3. What if a million or two women decided to stop complaining and start changing their lives!
4. What if a million or two women took full responsibility for their own happiness?
5. What if a million or two women really stopped waiting and stepped out?
6. What if a million or two women refused to allow anyone to measure their worth solely on their appearance?
7. What if a million or two women showed their loved ones they could renegotiate relationships and change their lives?

Self-reliance, self-esteem, self-respect, empowerment, conscious choices, speaking up - take whatever portion of the book you can use. Take it and use it in your life. As you do this, know that you are part of a movement which helps women establish internal permission to live prosperous and happy lives.

I've included three supplemental pages because I've been asked for them just about everywhere I go. The Wise Woman Credo is something my facilitator group and I worked out. The basic metaphysical ideas page first appeared in the facilitator training notebook and the leaders thought is was something which should be shared widely.

Dear reader, I trust you will find something of value in the book. I have found much of value in you and your responses.

Jane Claypool
Carlsbad, California
May 19, 1995

CHAPTER
ONE

_____

WISE WOMEN STEP OUT

It is 1944 and Jane is in the seventh grade in Wilmington, California. The oil well in the front of the school pumps day and night, the oil refineries emit strong and sometimes horrible smells in intermittent waves and the shipyard whistles blow for shift changes, coffee breaks, and send esoteric messages to the workers. Wilmington residents keep time by those whistles just as villagers in the Middle Ages marked their lives by the church bells. World War II is winding down and Jane is into puberty.

Jane is tall, blonde and pretty enough but already too smart, too forthright and too obstinate to please the people around her. A thoughtful child - Jane sees that life is complex and that she is going to have to keep her wits about her.

1

On Friday afternoons Jane and her classmates gather for the seventh-grade dances in the school gymnasium/auditorium. The dances are run by two old schoolteachers who volunteer their time to teach social graces. They are appalled by their students' upbringing and the seventh graders are appalled by their teachers' age and nonsensical ideas about deportment.

One of the teachers - Mrs. Gerstle - plays the piano. When pushed too hard, Mrs. Gerstle will collapse into a fountain of tears and go running home. While this is entertaining, the students really need her because the phonograph is broken. Therefore, the game becomes one of keeping her on the verge of hysteria without actually allowing her to gush open. The game breaks down about one in every three Friday afternoons.

The other teacher is made of sterner stuff, and Jane believes that is because Mrs. Peymiller teaches mathematics which is a much "harder" subject than music. Jane hates mathematics but she likes Mrs. Peymiller and is amused that this tiny woman who is in her late sixties (and came out of retirement during the war to teach for the war effort) can keep everyone in line. Mrs. Gerstle can only cry and run home but Mrs. Peymiller has found the secret to power and Jane slyly studies the older woman. How does she do it?

It is Mrs. Peymiller who organizes everything, lining the students up, announcing the dances and making the decision about the exact point when Bobby Brown is finally so bad that he must leave.

2

The rules are very clear. The boys must ask the girls to dance. *The girls must sit and wait.* There is a mad scramble for a few "cute" girls. The boys who lose the race, either through slowness or shyness, must be constantly prodded into action.

The girls who are not prizes are told to sit quietly, ankles (not legs) crossed and hands folded in laps. *Girls must wait.* Since this is a volunteer after-school activity there are many more girls than boys. *Many girls wait and wait and wait.*

Every Friday afternoon Jane goes to the dances and *waits* - a little terrified and thrilled at the same time. Who will choose her? Will it be one of the cute "bad boys" or will it be one of the "nice smart boys" who somehow don't count?

In the seventh grade, Jane has already learned that anything exciting that happens to her is supposed to happen *through* a male. Since Jane is constituted to want things to happen in her life, she has developed a taste for persons of the opposite sex who are discipline problems. Her favorite movie stars are tough guys Humphrey Bogart and Alan Ladd. At night, she practices doing her hair over one eye like Veronica Lake so she will be more attractive to Alan Ladd if she ever meets him.

Jane learns the two step, the waltz, the schottische, and the polka. Later, she will learn to jitterbug on her own because, in those days, nice girls didn't do it.

****

Waiting is a central theme in the lives of many women and girls even in our modern age. It certainly played a very great part in the ideas and beliefs that women of my generation were taught. Unfortunately, too many of us are still inclined to wait instead of taking charge of our lives, despite the clear evidence that waiting doesn't work very well after you graduate from seventh grade.

This book is written for women who are willing to graduate into a new way of living - one that claims greater freedom of choice, greater freedom of expression and greater freedom to be one's self. It is a combination of ideas which I have put together from the women's movement, metaphysics and observing the lives of extraordinary women.

Each chapter starts with an episode from my own life. Sometimes the episodes show success and sometimes they illustrate how far from the mark it is possible to stray. I wanted to share my own experience, my own hope and my own wisdom with women who are travelling on the same wonderful spiritual pathway.

I chose to share a portion of my personal story because I believe we each have a unique wisdom to share and that wisdom must be personal in order to be authentic.

My claim to wisdom comes from my courage to grow, my serenity to accept and my ability to know when to let something or someone go. As I have moved along Wisdom's highway, I have sometimes felt that my life was very, very different from most other women's. Now that I am older and wiser, I recognize that many of the conflicts in my personal life are universal themes for women of the 20th century.

Waiting is a basic theme. More and more, I am aware of how passive I was as a young woman despite the fact that I was told over and over that I was too aggressive, too pushy and too different. Only as I moved out of the cultural norms and began insisting on knowing myself did I come to a place in consciousness where I was willing to begin to take charge of my thinking and therefore, my life. I am still in process, of course. This plane of existence is clearly about being in process.

Learning to take control of my own life has included dealing with poverty, lack of opportunity, sexual and emotional abuse as a child, widowhood, and alcoholism as well as issues which centered around gender.

With a lot of help from others, I have moved from despair to joy, from misery to happiness and from isolation to a sure and certain knowledge that I am constantly supported by God.

Along the way, I have been a successful parent and grandparent, a successful teacher and writer and now I am a minister in a wonderful church which I founded.

As a minister, I have been privileged to teach Science of Mind, the philosophy which gave me the foundation to acquire wisdom. The ideas of Science of Mind can be found in most modern psychology and self-help books as well as from and many motivational leaders. I have presented these ideas in this book in very general terms, using the word *metaphysics*. You will probably recognize most of the ideas from other books and tapes you have encountered. What I hope will be unique will be the focus on women's lives and women's issues.

I am deeply grateful for the love and support which I encountered along Wisdom's pathway. In a very real sense, this book is an attempt to pay back to the Universe a portion of what I have gained.

So how do we recognize when we are playing a waiting game? Whenever we are deferring to another person's wishes, hoping someone will lend us the courage or support to change, or are repeating patterned behavior because someone in authority told us this was the way to do it, we are playing a waiting game.

Because we were taught so young and so thoroughly that we should wait until some one chooses us, many of us have never completely claimed control of our own lives.

Playing the passive Princess might have worked all right for the Friday afternoon dances but it doesn't work well at all in real life. Most women need to learn how to be more self-directive, more self-reliant and more self-confident. We can do this by using metaphysical principles and becoming aware of the challenges and the issues in our lives.

Wise Women of all generations are in the process of inventing themselves and shaping their lives in ways that seem to provide the most advantages, pleasure, and opportunities in today's world. They are ready to stop waiting for something to happen and do something to make it happen.

Wise Women understand that, at the level of political choice, they have more power than ever before. They are stepping out and insisting on equality in the work place, they are moving into politics and other power positions with aplomb. But truly Wise Women want more than political power - they want better personal lives as well.

It is not a question of getting power, it is a question of using the power that you already have. The central message of this book is that you don't have to wait any longer - you already have the power to take actions which will lead to a happier, healthier, more productive life. You are not stuck!

Once you recognize that you are working with Universal Power and that you use it by creating new thought patterns, you are on your way to understanding what a wonderful place you are at right now. You are on the edge of a new way of living. You are on the edge of opportunity and you don't have to wait for anyone else to choose you, help you, guide you or prod you into positive action. You can step out and dance through life right here and now.

Exercising your God-given power doesn't mean you have to live alone or be so independent you qualify for

Clint Eastwood's understudy. It means you can move in the direction of getting what you want in life - whether that includes a good relationship with another person or a trip to the Galapagos Islands. You set the goals, you train your thoughts and you take the actions.

Whether you are 26 or 86, whether you are married or single, lesbian or straight, celibate or in a committed relationship, you are in charge of you own life. You are making choices. You are making decisions and with a little different focus, those choices and decisions can be absolutely wonderful.

I define wisdom as being completely conscious of your own power and using it in loving (especially self-loving) ways. The important word here is loving.

Many books written for women describe a generic paralysis and want to place the blame on men (the generic oppressors). This is neither loving, appropriate, accurate, nor sensible. If we sit around and blame men, we are still just sitting around.

A spiritual view of life says that men and women are equal in their ability to create their lives. While we may have different circumstances and different cultural conditioning around gender issues, we can all access the same Universal Power. This power has absolutely nothing to do with gender - it is universal, creative and intelligent and it is equally accessible to all.

Books written about women's lives, whether in psychological or political language, tell the truth when they say, "Cinderella, it ain't going to happen, so hop out of the ashes and start designing your own pumpkin patch."

I meet a lot of women who are unconsciously waiting for someone else to do the work for them. Either they want their husbands to change so they can be happy or they want some man to "choose" them so they can be happy. Some are happy enough at home but find the workplace a frustrating maze.

These troubled women I see come in all ages. Whether they are 20 or 30 or 60, they are throwbacks to an ancient age. They are garden-variety females who were taught that their worth would be established through giving and receiving love. Unfulfilled, they wile away their lives, paddling into and out of jobs which don't pay much, drifting in and (hopefully) out of relationships which tell them they aren't good for much, dreaming of the day when some strong, attractive man will make it all right.

If you find you are waiting in any area of your life, you can change a core belief and live a more fulfilled life. This book is designed to help you do that.

In order to change, you will have to give up the idea that you are a victim. You will have to take charge of your thinking and you will have to identify exactly what you want. You can do all of those things. In order to truly emerge into a full and happy life, you will have to begin to take responsibility for making wise choices now.

As a Wise Woman, you can stop seeing yourself as a victim and let go of blaming villains. You can recognize yourself as the heroine in your own spiritual journey. You are the star of your life and you can love and admire yourself. All this is possible when we begin to take charge of our choices and stop waiting.

As a Wise Woman, I am having fun. I am usually having too much fun to explain, to complain, to worry or sing the blues. I am simply starring in my own life and that is enough. I want the same sense of exhilaration for you. I want you to be able to say with me, "I am Power. I am Love. I am Freedom. I am Wise."

****

QUESTIONS

1. What was your first introduction to the waiting game?

2. Do you see places in your life where you are still waiting?

3. Can you imagine asking anyone to dance today?

4. How do you avoid rejection and take risks? Do you see any patterns you would like to change?

5. Are there ideas from the past which no longer serve you?

AFFIRMATIONS

I dance to my own tune.

The beat I keep is to my own drummer.

I am dancing through life, having a wonderful time.

My past is fascinating and fun. It does not control me.

I am having fun now.

I don't wait - I use my power now.

CHAPTER
TWO

WISE WOMEN WRITE
THEIR OWN SCRIPTS

It is 1951. Jane is 18 years old, married and very pregnant. She is not sure exactly how it all happened but she remembers she was in love and wanted to get married. Now that she is married, she sees it doesn't have to have much to do with love. It seems to have more to do with housework, staying home with a grumpy husband and feeling trapped. She is a little angry at herself for not figuring it out in advance, because all the other women she knows feel trapped but somehow, she thought she would escape. She thought her husband would be different. She thought she would have an exciting life, although she can't remember why.

Her belly dismays her. Jane knows what it means to be certain you were unwanted and she is determined that will never be an issue for her child. On the other hand, 18 is very, very young.

Her husband, who is in college, brings his debate partner home to cook a real curry dinner for them. The debate partner is from India and he wears a turban. After preparing the dinner, the young Sikh confesses he has never cooked before in his life. In India, he slept on silk sheets and had servants. Here in America he eats in restaurants.

He then claims he can read palms and proceeds to read Jane's hand. He says she has a thumb which denotes stubbornness and sensuality. Her husband is annoyed and says she should go to the kitchen and wash the dishes now. She does as she's told, but not for long.

****

Like you, I came into this life with a strong hunger for personal freedom. It was a part of my personality or "original essence" and my need for freedom was in decided combat with society in the 1950s. My determination to be myself, and later, to be self-reliant, went unnamed, intermittently buried, constantly misunderstood - but it never really died out.

I was a girl who wanted to be loved, growing into a woman who wanted to be herself, and in that sense, my story is every woman's story. I sensed that I was expected to play a part in this great carnival of life. I also saw that people wore lots of different masks and

14

that the lines they spoke weren't necessarily what they really meant. Like many children, I was quite intuitive and I was honest. I was also very, very confused.

At this point in my life, I believe that my desire for individual liberty is my natural divinity, but in those days I just thought of it as a painful part of my unreconstructed personality. My need to choose my own destiny was a toothache which simply wouldn't go away. Whenever I bit into something sweet, the pain would follow.

Like most women my age, I have spent a lifetime balancing the goal of freedom with another important goal - love. It seems to me that the great *koan* of contemporary Western women's lives is exactly that. How do I have love and freedom?

In the 1930s and 1940s, when I was growing up, the choices presented to women were very narrow and frightened me. I had an innate desire to live a life different from the one I saw my mother and grandmother and aunts living. They were obviously unhappy and seemed trapped; I had a voice within me which insisted there must be a different way. I looked to the movies for guidance, just as young people from today's dysfunctional families look to television. We shudder when we think of a generation of young women raised with the values they learned on *Roseanne*, but things haven't changed much.

I watched movies which taught me that if a young woman had blonde hair and chewed gum (Gloria

Graham, Joan Blondell, and Shelley Winters) it was very likely she would die before the last reel. Those same movies portrayed gentle, loving women (Donna Reed) as the ones who earned love and lived happily ever after with biscuits on the table and pot roast in the oven. They sang in kitchens while their contented husbands relaxed with a newspaper in the living room. My trouble was that I preferred reading the newspaper to cooking.

I learned that to be loved by a powerful man was the most desirable outcome possible for a woman's life. I also learned that men had power and women shouldn't.

It was really very simple. The good girl got the hero. The good girl didn't have many opinions but she loved the hero.

The good girl didn't have many lines in the movie either. She would stand on the porch waving a handkerchief as the men rode off to <u>do something.</u> Usually, she would reappear in the last reel as she ran to greet the conquering hero. Occasionally she had to nurse him back to health. Once in a while she was tied to the railroad tracks and she had to look helpless as that mean old train bore down on her semi-bared bosom.

No matter what the plot was, it was the hero who did the acting. The good girl sat very still, looking very pretty, and waited to be discovered. If she had large breasts and a blank expression the chances were good that some nice fellow would come along and love her. Then she would bake biscuits happily ever after!

****

QUESTIONS

1. What nonsense were you taught as a girl?

2. Does that nonsense stand in your way today?

3. What could you believe instead?

4. What dreams of exciting activities would you like to dust off and take out of the closet?

AFFIRMATIONS

I write my own lines and my own script.

I am the star of my own life.

My life is successful and fun.

I love myself and I am well loved.

My life is fun and exciting.

CHAPTER
THREE

WISE WOMEN
ARE CREATIVE

It is 1938. Jane is five years old. She is taking a very long drive into the Ozark Mountains with her father. The leaves are red, orange, and yellow and the sun appears and disappears in surprising shafts of brilliance as the car goes round and round the hills. Jane is drowsy and when the car stops she is disturbed because she would rather sleep. Her father leads her up a dirt slope and they go onto the porch of a wooden house.

Jane has never seen a house as poor as this one. It reminds her of a hillbilly comic strip called Barney Google. She knows that the people who live in this house must be very, very poor and she is curious about how that feels. "You stay out here with the little girl," her father says.

The man who is talking to her father says, "Her name is Mary." Her father and the man go inside the house. Jane is left outside.

The girl on the porch is about ten, with long, straight brown hair and pale skin. She has long, thin legs and arms and pale blue eyes with circles under them. The girl has a ragged dress on and no shoes. She does not look up at Jane or acknowledge that she knows Jane is there. Jane sits down on the porch step and watches the girl as she opens a cigar box and takes out some papers.

The girl hands Jane one of the papers and says, "You be Mary. I be Janie."

Jane looks down at the paper in her hand and realizes that it is a figure of a young girl cut from a magazine. The young girl is wearing cotton underwear. "Are these your paper dolls?" Jane asks.

"I cut them from Sears," the girl answers proudly.

Jane thinks of her own collection of paper dolls. They include a full set of Queen Elizabeth dolls with bright colored wigs and fancy dresses. All her paper dolls come from the five and dime store and the figures are cardboard so they are easier to make stand up.

Jane loves to make up stories so she begins the game by saying, "Let's pretend we take a walk and see a castle...."

That day, on that ramshackle porch, she plays a good game of paper dolls even though the figures are only wearing underwear and they flop over if you try and hold them too straight.

When Jane's father comes out of the house, Mary gives her one of her treasured figures. Jane and her father drive away. Even though it is late, the sun is still lighting the backs of the trees. Jane is transported into a new sense of possibility by that game of paper dolls and from that moment on, light and color are fused with imagination in her mind. She will always think of light as being full of creative possibility.

Jane loses the figure very quickly but she never loses the real gift. From that time on, she understands that imagination needs very few props to bring pleasure.

****

Imagination is a precious gift which we need to nurture and develop no matter how old we are. We use imagination in our adult lives just as well as when we are children. The beauty of being an adult is that you can actually move in the direction your imagination takes you. You are not limited to "only make believe." You can harness your creative power and make it work for you.

Imagination is a crucial ingredient in shaping a life you really want to experience. How can you know what kind of choices to make if you don't have enough imagination to know what you want?

Actually, imagination is a God-given attribute and we all have plenty of potential for exercising our creative minds. Some of us may need to develop confidence in shaping our dreams but once we give ourselves internal permission, we will regain that childlike ability to move into the world of creative mind play.

All great activities begin with a vision. The woman who invented the wheel probably had a good idea what she wanted before she started chopping the edges off that square rock. We follow the promptings of our imagination when we redesign our home, when we choose our vacation destination and when we select our college major.

Before we marry, we imagine we have chosen the best possible mate. Most of us even use our imagination when we name our children. Surely the woman who names her daughter Elizabeth has a different creative vision than the woman who names her daughter Autumn Branch and they are both quite different from the woman who names her daughter Venus.

Before you can make much progress in taking charge of your life and making choices which create changes, you will have to create a vision of what you really do want. Some women have been so ensnared by cultural boundaries that they honestly have trouble knowing what they want in their lives. They live in the house their husband selected, wear the clothes their mother said were flattering and listen to the music their friends like. They go to lunch with friends and wait until someone orders something they like. Then they say, "I'll have the same."

Rather than create a life based on someone else's specifications, wouldn't you rather develop your own dreams? You can do it. Life will actually shape itself around your dreams if you can envision them clearly enough and open your mind and heart to the possibilities. Visionary ability is the basis of practical metaphysics.

If you feel as though you don't use your imagination enough or as though your imagination is very limited, you might want to undertake some activities to renew your acquaintance with the creative child-mind which is inside you all the time.

Try keeping a dream journal. Put a pad and pencil beside your bed and make it a practice to write your dreams down the first thing in the morning. You will quickly discover that there is a part of you which is full of fun and alive and well. This child-mind dreams in puns, symbols and even jokes about your daily activities. It will also bring you very deep intuitive messages if you begin listening.

You might also try some free association activities in your regular daytime journal. Take a word such as family or Thanksgiving and put it in the middle of the page. Then allow yourself three minutes to come up with as many words and phrases as you can. Don't critique the ideas, just let them flow.

Daydreaming to good music is very relaxing and easy for a lot of people. It might help if you set aside a certain time each day and select some harmonious and pleasant composition to listen to. Close your eyes and let your mind wander. If you can't get beyond tomorrow's

TO DO list, try imagining that you are in a wonderful pool of water and there is a waterfall behind you. Let the water and music carry you where it will.

For many people, making lists of their goals is an easy way to daydream. I think goals are important but they have to be approached with caution. Goals can be used as just more evidence that we don't measure up to the mark. Goals can also be so vague that they distract from the necessary work you must do in order to move on in life. Some women become their most rigid selves when they write goals and the list quickly looks as though it were written by the meanest boss in the world.

Imagination should be fun. So should visionary work. Try writing a "blue sky list" for a whole week, covering page after page with possibilities. Just fill in anything that looks like it might be fun (even for the moment). Write, "Buy a diamond bracelet," and let that sit beside "Build an adobe house," or "Wear a feathered headdress." No comments - no judgment, just creative mind-play.

After a week of fooling around with ideas, certain themes will emerge. You can consider them as possibilities for action at some point. If they seem unattainable right now, don't worry about it. Just file them away in your "life plan" folder. Someday I plan to go to Africa. I'm not sure how that will fit in with my generally busy schedule but I don't worry about it. I just keep the African trip in my "life plan" file. When I'm ready, the vision is there.

When you daydream, what do you wish for? Those dreams are clues to your deepest desires. Ask yourself if your daydreams reflect a sense of yourself as an actor in your life or if they center around someone else bringing everything you desire.

Use your daydreams to approach core beliefs which you want to change. If you want to become very recognized in your work, why not daydream about standing on a podium and getting lots of applause for what you've done? If you find your daydreams all center around someone else bringing what you want into your life, you might want to deliberately design some new daydreams to enjoy part of the time. For instance, if you consistently dream of marrying a rich man, why not vary the program by dreaming of getting a big promotion or starting your own business.

Daydreams can be fun and reinforce our positive choices in our daily lives. You don't have to repeat a trillion versions of Cinderella or Snow White just because of your early programming. You are not a computer, you are an imaginative person.

Experiment with playing the lead role in *Indiana Jones* instead of the part of the screaming bimbo. Your mind is a free country and you don't have to wait for central casting to put you in the starring part. How about playing Princess Charming and the Sleeping Prince?

Our imaginations are the key to establishing a higher vision for our lives. We can move into a world of greater possibility through the choices we make, but first, we must be able to imagine being in that desired space.

You may be limiting yourself by your inability to imagine being the CEO or your inability to imagine yourself in a happy marriage or your inability to imagine yourself in a size 10 dress. Learn to work with your imagination. It is the key to change.

****

QUESTIONS

1. What was your favorite kind of imagination game as a child?

2. What are your memories around making up stories?

3. Do you consciously use your imagination now?

4. What is the most imaginative thing you did last week?

5. What kinds of creative activities do you engage in now?

AFFIRMATIONS

I am creative and talented.

I have a wonderful, creative, and ingenious mind.

I have great ideas.

I have a wonderful vision for my future.

My imagination is my private, positive territory. I stake my claim on the gold.

CHAPTER
FOUR

WISE WOMEN SEEK SUCCESS

It is 1948. Jane is 15 years old. She is the winner in the district finals of the Los Angeles City Schools Speech Contest. She is now on stage, giving her speech at the regional level. The judges at the district level are so sure she will win that she has been told to bring a packed bag to the contest. She will fly to Sacramento right after she wins the contest tonight.

Jane has never flown before and her bag is not packed. There is a belief in her home that you shouldn't count your chickens before they are hatched.

Jane is doing a great job on her talk about James Madison and his role in founding a democratic nation. She has the talk perfectly memorized - the pauses and the dramatic inflections are there on schedule. Mr. Sklar, her speech teacher, has worked all year to help her lower her voice, saying that high women's voices are annoying on public platforms. She knows her voice is acceptable and she feels just fine about her performance.

She is on the last paragraph - she looks out at the audience and sees her boyfriend who is a speech major in college. She sees her mother and sister who are sitting right up front, looking worried for her.

She goes blank.... The last paragraph of the speech disappears completely from her mind. She stands there - looking at absolute blackness for thirty seconds and then she says, "I've forgotten," and walks off stage.

She does not cry but she goes numb - delaying the pain of failure indefinitely by simply not feeling anything. It is a stoic pattern which is labeled brave and gains her admiration - a sort of consolation prize for not winning the big one. Later, one judge tells her she would have won anyway if she'd simply walked away and said nothing.

Everyone is very nice to her, especially the boy who will be going to Sacramento! Her mother is especially loving and tells her not to mind, that they all love her anyway. Her boyfriend takes her out for ice cream. She does not speak publicly again for many, many years.

****

Fear of success is a common phenomenon among women. It is learned early, and many women never really overcome the conscious or subconscious belief that if they are too successful, they will not be loved.

Since women are taught from the day they arrive on this planet that their worth comes from their ability to attract and hold the admiration and love of others, many do not even think of going directly after success in a public way. They approach success very obliquely. They raise their sons to become President of the United States or they marry men who will produce the world's best movie or build the world's highest bridge. They stand in the wings and clap as their loved ones accept prizes. Usually, the loved ones have the grace to mention them in their acceptance speeches.

While many women have jobs, only a few have successful careers. To go directly after success in business, in the creative arts, or in education is still a rare approach to life for a woman. It takes commitment, ambition, and a lot of energy. Many women simply make other choices.

At this point in history, most women are more comfortable in a supportive role and there's nothing really wrong with that, as long as they are making conscious choices. A baseball team needs nine players and only one can be the pitcher.

Whatever we do to live prosperous, happy, life-affirming lives is all right. There never has been anything at all wrong with being a housewife, a nurse, a schoolteacher or a junior partner in the family business. The difficulty comes when we play a supporting role and resent it. It is the resentment which poisons our lives, not the particular roles we choose.

Wherever there is resentment or jealousy about not being recognized or not being successful, I suspect there is a failure to accept responsibility for not going after what we want. We may not always get everything we want in life, but it is almost certain we won't get anything we want if we can't identify and state our desires.

I taught school off and on, for a total of seventeen years from 1956 until 1981, and in every one of my eight schools, the principal was a man. When a few opportunities were opened to women, many of the best women hesitated to go for the extra credentials they needed. In some cases they were happier in the classroom, in other cases they didn't want the responsibility, but in most cases, they just couldn't step out and say, "I want to be boss."

Our society says it is natural for men to speak more, take charge faster and assert themselves in the world of work. Some women are already working on asserting themselves more and speaking up more. Other women are standing back and saying, "Oh I couldn't do that." Still others are waiting and looking around for role models who present a healthy, well-balanced life as success.

One of the political issues in the women's movement has centered around whether the only "real" success must come from following male models. Should women climb the corporate ladder and forego childbearing to prove they are successes? Is joining the country club and learning to play golf going to pay off in business if you would rather read a book? Most women have had the good sense to say, "Of course not."

The navy blue suit with white blouse and bright red scarf worn as a necktie may have been the dress for success model of the seventies, but most women simply didn't want to wear navy blue suits all their lives.

There is a middle ground and, as a group, we are finding it. In the meantime, there is a lot of silly advice, a lot of silly anger, and a lot of silly posturing going on. Few of us look like Connie Chung. Few of us want to entertain like Martha Stewart and few of us want to emulate Barbara Bush or Hillary Clinton.

So what is success in today's world? Success is what you say it is. It may be that the life you are currently leading is very successful and you know it. Or it may be that you want to change your relationship to the world in order to feel more successful. Or it may be that you are already doing what you want, but you are in the habit of thinking of what you are doing as failure. In that case, all you need to change is your definition of success.

If you are feeling resentment toward others, toward the system or even toward yourself, you have some work to do on success. You probably need to ask yourself if you are afraid to go after what you want. You certainly need to ask yourself what you want. If your answers seem clogged with other people's opposition, then take a look at yourself and see if you have a core belief that you need to get your feeling of success from other people's approval.

If you don't know what you want and you don't know what success would look like, begin to do some inner work which will help you decide. Writing out the answers to the questions in this book will be a strong beginning. Check the bibliography for other books you might read. Start a no-commitment list in your journal where you simply jot down things you think you might like to do or be. Allow yourself the freedom to write anything at all down without feeling you have to follow through on it. Just allow yourself to speak up and express and see what develops.

In workshops, I ask people to say out loud what they really want in life. There is no responsibility attached to this exercise, just acknowledging their desires is enough for the exercise. Many people have a very hard time saying, "I want to retire at 50," or "I want to remarry," or "I want to be promoted to general manager of my branch."

Acknowledging that we want things is the very first step in taking responsibility for going after what we want. Many women are so unaccustomed to thinking in terms of their own needs and desires that it is a major breakthrough for them to say, "I want to go to the Bahamas instead of fishing in Canada this year." If that takes so much energy - imagine the energy it takes to book a flight!

Be kind to yourself and stop insisting that everything needs to change right away. Often, in the beginning of our consciousness-raising work, we think we have to make much more drastic adjustments than we really have to make. As we go through the steps of self-discovery, we find we've been doing pretty well all along. Some minor adjustments are probably all that are necessary. In fact, we can probably call ourselves a success right here and now!

Be aware of how much you are blaming others for your problems. Are you wasting your time and energy on resentment? Is there someone in your life who you believe stops your every attempt at moving into a higher level of success?

As long as you are blaming others for your inaction and unhappiness, you are not using your full power. You are using anger to mask your own fear of stepping out into the world and becoming self-reliant.

Keeping quiet and resenting often appears easier than facing fear of being alone or fear of not being loved. But resentment poisons life. Both the women's movement and metaphysical teaching agree that it is better to step out and speak up than to sulk in the corner.

Fear of success seems to be just another way in which we try to give away our God-given power. If I believe that being the school principal means success for me, I should go for it. I should forget the arguments that it is harder for a woman to be promoted and I should go back to school and get the credentials.

Actually getting prepared for the next step tells the Universe you are ready. After you are prepared, be sure and tell your bosses! Let them know that you are ready, willing and able. If you are passed over, come back the next year and tell them again.

Take a pro-active approach and you will get the promotion. Sulk in the corner and you will be miserable. Thoughts are often no more than habit patterns and one nasty habit that many women have is to go over and over the lack of opportunity they face. Often, this is based on old information. Even if it is not, the women who are complaining need to ask themselves if they are emotionally and intellectually prepared for the promotion.

A woman who prepares herself emotionally and intellectually for success will achieve it. Just getting an MBA won't guarantee a fast rise in the business world, you must also be emotionally ready to take responsibility for making big decisions and be willing to delegate minor tasks. You must be able and willing to speak up without sounding angry or conciliatory. You must be able to speak the language of the big league if you really want to play with the big leagues.

Wearing a suit, earning a lot of money, and working long hours is not the picture of success for every women and that's fine. We are free to define our own success and copying male models doesn't really work for most of us. We can invent our own ways of being - sharing power, building co-operative partnerships, working in our own homes, all kinds of major innovations are already in the wind. There are myriad models, many are healthier than the ones we see on the cover of Forbes Magazine.

My point is simply this - to blame others for your failure is futile. Define what success is for you and prepare yourself thoroughly for that success. Go for it.

****

QUESTIONS

1. Am I blaming anyone else for my troubles?

2. Do I believe I am a failure or a success now?

3. What would increased success look and feel like to me now?

4. How much energy am I putting into pleasing people? On a scale of 1 to 10, where do I put myself?

AFFIRMATIONS

I accept success as my birthright.

I am willing to change and grow.

I am willing to be successful right now.

I measure my success by what I think and do.

CHAPTER
FIVE

WISE WOMEN
ARE WILLING TO RISK

It is 1955. Jane is 22 years old. She is in college, studying elementary education and hating every minute of it. The classes are boring and she doesn't really want to teach elementary school anyway. She is only taking the course because she needs to get out of college quickly and support herself and her child.

She works 30 hours a week and takes a full schedule at college. She doesn't study much and she hangs out a lot in the student commons talking and drinking coffee or sometimes she goes to the record library and listens to old Folkways albums of blues singers. She has memorized all of Leadbelly's lyrics by the time her first term at Long Beach State is half over.

School isn't difficult, just tedious and much of her unhappiness has to do with her personal problems. There are days when she feels as if she is on a slow motion treadmill and will never get off. When will her real life begin? When will she be free of her parents and her need for their help? When will she be able to really say that she's recovered from the death of her young husband? When WILL she actually be in a position to make a home for herself and her daughter?

She is required to take an exploratory art course and it is the only bright spot in her week. She really likes the professor, who is from the University of Chicago and not used to California at all. He blinks a lot in the sunshine and makes comments about things Jane takes for granted. He likes to go to restaurants built in the shape of hot dogs or oranges. His name is Simon Steiner and he makes wry little observations about California life. She sometimes has the feeling that he is as lost as she is, though for very different reasons.

One day, Mr. Steiner invites his whole class to the Long Beach Pike to explore photography. Only three students actually show up and Jane is one of them. They walk up and down the Pike, taking photographs of garbage cans, rims of the Ferris wheel, drunks left over from the night before and the texture of the wooden benches. For the first time in a very long time, Jane feels interested in school and in life. She is having fun.

They stop for hot dogs and Jane says she's enjoyed the day very much.

"You're quite talented. You should be going to school on the east coast, you know," Mr. Steiner says.

Jane laughs. "I'll be lucky to get through Long Beach State."

"You could get a scholarship, I'm certain you could," he persists.

"I have a daughter," she tells her teacher. She thinks he already knows that but perhaps he's forgotten.

"You could leave her with your mother," Mr. Steiner suggests. "I could get you a place to live with friends of mine. My wife has a cousin who'd give you a room. You should be in a good school, you really should."

Jane shakes her head and goes over to buy herself a beer. She doesn't care if it is only 12 in the morning. She's old enough to drink. No one appears to notice as she returns to the table with her beer.

Mr. Steiner sighs and says, "California is all right but you really deserve a better education. You're too bright and too talented."

Jane shrugs. "I have to get out of school as fast as I can."

"What will you do then?"

"Teach elementary school."

He shakes his head. "You could at least teach art in a high school."

"I'm majoring in elementary education because it only takes four years. Look, all I want is a piece of paper with my name on it. Then I can get a job and I'll be all right."

He looks as if there are a lot of things he might say but all he says is, "You could switch to an art major. They'll give you a special credential in art and you can get your job."

"Are you sure I can get out in four years? I only have two to go."

"Yes."

"I'll do it." Jane finishes the beer and tosses it in the garbage can.

****

Taking risks is very difficult for some women but most successful people find that the ability to take risks is a part of their ability to build a successful life. Some of us were taught to be so frightened of change that we have a hard time switching grocery stores. Others take risks only when things are so bad that the pain overcomes the fear. There is a better way to live.

Taking risks can be fun. It certainly is a way to improve upon the original design of your life and it can alleviate major problems. While it looked whimsical to the people who were advising me, my choice to move from elementary education to art education probably saved me from dropping out of school altogether.

I didn't turn into a great artist. I didn't even stay in art education very long, but I've never regretted the switch. It moved me into a brand new exciting field of activity and into the company of people I liked much more. I was a better fit in the art department than I was in elementary education and that made all the difference. I'm glad I took the risk.

Taking risks always implies that you might lose something and like most risk takers, I've lost a few times. On the whole, risk taking has paid off for me because I moved in a direction that appeared to be a better one. If I were to critique my life, I'd say I got into more trouble by hanging on than by jumping in. Most mature women would probably say the same thing.

The saddest people I've ever known were the ones who wanted to do something very much and never could find the courage to try it. My dearest uncle dreamed of acting all his life but he never quite had the courage to take the risk. He lingered painfully on the edge of that conflict. As the years caught up with him, he became sadder and sadder. He moved from <u>wanna be</u> to <u>never has been</u> without ever even knowing if he might have made the big time.

Even if you don't get exactly what you aim for, it is wonderful to step out and reach for that star. The writer who spends her life trying to write the great American novel and ends up writing copy for the back of cereal boxes usually doesn't resent life. She went for something and learned a great deal about herself in the process. Besides, what's wrong with writing cereal box copy if it is a good cereal?

It is the aspiring writer who doesn't write, who blames "those New Yorkers" or blames her kids for taking up all her time, or blames her need to work at a full-time job who falls into resentment and self-pity about her unfulfilled talent. Putting blame on others doesn't work in any area of our lives.

Once we really get it that we have the power to make positive choices, then we begin to understand how little risk is really involved in risk taking. If I hate my job, what is the real risk involved in leaving it? If I'm in a bad relationship and I spend all my time wishing I were elsewhere, what's the risk in going elsewhere?

****

QUESTIONS

1. Do you consider yourself a risk taker?

2. What risks have you taken that worked well?

3. Are there any risks you've taken which didn't work? What was the eventual outcome of the change you made?

AFFIRMATIONS

I exercise my positive power to create a great life.

I have wonderful choices and I make some new ones every day.

I love to make positive changes in my life.

Fear isn't in my vocabulary. I am a brave woman.

CHAPTER
SIX

WISE WOMEN KNOW THERE IS A POWER FOR GOOD WORKING IN THEIR LIVES

It is 1953. Jane is 20 years old. She is standing in the window of the store where she is working, decorating for Christmas. She is told there is a telephone call for her.

Jane goes to the telephone and her brother-in-law tells her, "Dennis is dead."

"Thank you," Jane says and puts the telephone down in the cradle. She has been expecting the call - has known for several weeks that her young husband was fatally ill - but even so, she is not emotionally prepared.

She calls her father who sends his cousin to drive her home. On the way, the cousin offers her a drink and some advice, "Get remarried as fast as you can. Pretty girl like you will find a father for her kid fast."

She takes the drink. The advice is unthinkable but over the next ten years she will hear it again and again.

She goes through the next two days and the funeral in a daze, letting the older people do whatever they think is best. She is in no condition to make decisions and she has never felt more alone, more vulnerable and more isolated in her life.

To be a widow at twenty. To be without funds and without plans. To be the mother of a small child. To face the rest of her life without the man she planned to be married to forever. To face the rest of her life without the father of her child. To face the rest of her life without the person who had been her best friend all the way through her teen years. She can't begin to deal with any of it.

****

Feeling separate and isolated is a frightening condition and the alienation I felt as a child was compounded by the death of my first husband. For years, I would find no one and no place in which I could feel safe.

The older adults who surrounded me were almost callous in their assumption that I could simply remarry and make everything all right. How could I tell anyone

48

that I hadn't enjoyed being married and didn't plan to try it again? I wasn't even ready to admit it to myself.

My early twenties were nightmare years in many ways. I moved home to my parents' house and my mother and I quarreled constantly about everything. My father was drinking so much by then that living with him was very dangerous, yet it was my only apparent choice. I had to get through college and get a well-paying job if I were ever to be self-sufficient.

I did graduate at age twenty-three and I began teaching art in a junior high school. I did find a good school for my daughter and I found ways to give her a good education and a good self image.

When I almost killed myself in an automobile accident at age 26, I was able to quit drinking and stay sober for ten years. I was able to get good ratings at teaching and, when sober, establish successful relationships with nice men.

As I look back on those early years, I realize how close to disaster I skated. Guilt and shame were in the very air I breathed. Most of my actions were propelled by negative emotions and I made many, many wrong decisions. I had problems with my family and I certainly didn't deal with them intelligently. I even had a problem in college and almost didn't get my teaching credential because I was such a "party girl." Clearly, I was on the edge of disaster most of the time.

Yet, my goals were completed! I achieved my version of being a good parent, having good work and earning some financial security. Though I didn't think I believed in God, I often had the sense that something was helping me as I muddled through my confused life. It seemed that there were always people who liked me and who wanted to help. It seemed as though my love for my daughter overcame many of the difficulties we might have faced. It seemed as though every <u>clear</u> vision and every <u>clear</u> goal I could set for myself was achieved.

I know now that the first step in any kind of success is to have a clear goal. I did have goals and although I experienced much more struggle than might have been necessary if I had been wiser, I did stick with them.

Most of us would say things could have been easier for us if we were to take a look backward. But it is silly to look backward if your only purpose is regret. Life is about growth and change, and a successful life will always result in knowing more at maturity than at twenty.

I am glad I was wise enough to know that if you can see clearly what you want, you can usually achieve it. I could see clearly that I was going to have to be independent, self-reliant and self-supporting. Despite all the nonsense in my life, I never let go of those goals.

In metaphysics, we believe that the Universe (or God or Universal Intelligence) responds to clear-cut goals and intentions. Our actions are often a measure of how clear cut and definite our intentions are. In my case, my actions sent very confused messages to the Universe, but I was able to make enough right choices to move me in the right direction. In every case, when I made a clear cut decision to go after something, I got it. Usually, the Universe supplied a "lucky break" or an easier way for me to achieve my dreams.

It was not wishful thinking that made me think that there was something out there supporting my goals. Universal Power was the wind beneath my wings in every life-affirming choice I made.

The beginning of true wisdom is to understand that we are living in a world in which there is a Power For Good. What's more, that Power For Good is operating in our lives right now. We don't have to beg, plead, or repent in order to have God on our side. God is always on our side. God is not only on our side - God is all around us and in us. We are in a permanent, wonderful and circulating relationship with God.

When I began to study metaphysics, I was allergic to the word God. For me, at that time, the word brought up feelings of shame, guilt, fear and punishment. I found terms such as Divine Intelligence or Spiritual Law much easier to work with.

Once I really heard someone say out loud that there were Spiritual Laws responding to the messages we sent into the Universe, I understood what had been happening in my life. The "good stuff" and the "bad stuff" were simply responses to the messages I had been sending. If I changed the message, I could have more "good stuff" in my life.

51

This is a very simple explanation but it works. Try changing the messages you are giving the Universe and watch your life change rapidly. You are no longer a victim who has been pummeled and sculpted by Life - you are suddenly the sculptor, working with a powerful co-Creator. Your life begins to take the shape you desire and you understand the true meaning of the word freedom.

Every experience in our lives has a mental cause. Even such an apparently uncontrollable event as the death of a loved one carries opportunities to mold your own experience. When someone dies it is not necessary to go into a seven-year period of grief. The experience of isolation, grief and rage which I felt were a product of my belief system as much as of what happened. It is natural and normal to mourn the loss of a loved one, but it is neither natural nor necessary to take a self-destructive dive.

Wisdom teaches us that we have control and choices. Wisdom teaches us that we have the ability to live positive lives, no matter what kind of things happen to us. Wisdom increases our ability to pick and choose our emotions.

Most experiences are clearly a product of our choices and beliefs. For instance, if I am in a relationship where I am constantly being picked on, I am in that relationship because I have some belief which is being fulfilled. Maybe I think I deserve punishment, maybe I think I can feel good about myself by seeing that my partner is much worse than I am. Usually, the beliefs are more complicated than the ideas which appear in self-help books, but anyone who has read self-help books understands this concept.

Metaphysics goes beyond self-help books by looking at God as a Creative Energy which operates according to definite spiritual laws. This Creative Energy which we call Universal Mind, God, Higher Power, or simply, The Universe, must respond to our beliefs by producing what we believe in material form.

You don't have to define yourself as being a part of a particular religious belief to observe this happening in your life. Most women have heard the saying of Jesus in Matthew 21:22, "And all things ye shall ask in prayer, believing, ye shall receive." Most women are already familiar with similar concepts we find in self-help books and motivational seminars. These concepts are essentially correct.

Begin to notice how your belief system is reflected in your current life. Begin to notice how you would like to change your life and ask yourself which beliefs you would have to change in order to do this. For instance, if you notice you are spending entirely too much time worrying about making someone else happy, think about whether or not you believe it is your responsibility to make others happy. Can you change that belief to one which allows you to be happy and others to sign on for the program if they choose?

****

QUESTIONS

1. What goals have you set and successfully completed?

2. Did you feel as though you were getting help from the Universe as you worked on these goals?

3. How would you say you have gained in wisdom since your twenties?

4. Do you look backward and give yourself applause for doing so well? Try it!

AFFIRMATIONS

The Universe supports my choices.

I am surrounded and supported by God as I choose to move into success.

What I can conceive, I can achieve. I have terrific vision.

I am ready, willing and able to go for the best in my life.

I am centered in love and always supported by God, which is Love.

CHAPTER
SEVEN

WISE WOMEN
ARE REALLY BEAUTIFUL

It is 1938. Jane is five years old. She is looking at a newspaper clipping - a photograph of Jane in a bathing suit. She has just won a beauty contest. Her parents are laughing because she won instead of her beautiful little sister. They think the judges were fools.

Jane looks at her photo in bewilderment. Why has the newspaper made the mistake? If she could, she would tell them they gave the prize to the wrong girl and then her parents would stop laughing. She wants to put her hands over her ears. She never enjoys the family jokes and this laughter is especially painful.

To Jane, the image in the newspaper clipping is unrecognizable. That photo-Jane appears to be a healthy, sturdy little girl with straight blonde hair and very clear blue eyes. She looks quite competent and intelligent and older than her years.

So it will be all her life. She will look sturdy and healthy and strong. She will look as though she knows a great deal more than others. The child Jane will soon disappear and the photo-Jane who replaces her will find it nearly impossible to integrate the confusion, fear and self-doubt with the mirror handed her by society. She will grow apart from herself, distancing the pain but somehow knowing that her insides never quite match her outsides.

Jane must have been a beautiful baby. Objective authorities such as newspapers and judges are as trustworthy as interior reality, and certainly more trustworthy than parents.

In retrospect, it is clear that this is not an individual story entirely. Shirley Temple is mixed up in this matter. Little sister has curly hair and so does Shirley Temple.

****

All children are beautiful and you and I were absolutely gorgeous when we were born. We weren't born bad and we weren't born with the mark of Cain on us. We weren't born to live out some tacky karma and we weren't born to live a miserable life so we could get to heaven by and by.

We may have been born with temperaments and appearances which did not fit the idealized image our parents had in mind. We may not have exactly fit the culture's norms. We most certainly couldn't have fit the culture's idealized version of what a perfect child, perfect girl and perfect woman looked and acted like.

The unhappier our parents were with themselves, the more unhappy they probably were with us. The more concerned they were with appearances, the more we learned to look good and not let on what was going on behind the closed doors of our minds or our homes.

Many of us have developed an inner rating system which is based on idealized images that we could never hope to live up to. We go through life thinking we are ugly when we are really quite nice looking and could be beautiful if we smiled more. We go through life feeling like we are failures because we couldn't please chronically unhappy or out-of-touch parents.

Perhaps the most tragic thing that can happen to us is that we separate ourselves from our own emotions in order to please others, and we go through life pretending to be someone we are not. Image becomes more important than reality. Image becomes so real that we aren't even sure we are in there.

Reality checks are always useful. Look around you at the successful, happy people who are not perfect image fits. Did Eleanor Roosevelt look like the perfect President's wife? Does Barbra Streisand sing worse because she has a big nose? Is Marilyn Monroe fat in 1956 or just by 1995 standards? Are size 9 feet big? Who says 6 feet is too tall? Has Linda Hunt's acting career been ruined because she is 4-something-feet?

No matter what nonsense we may have picked up as children, we can believe something different now. We can stop judging ourselves by imaginary standards, stop blaming our parents for saying we weren't good enough and we can start looking at life with a little wisdom.

It isn't your fault your ears stick out but it is up to you whether or not you let it ruin your life. Buy big earrings! Let your hair grow long and have your teeth capped. Life will work out.

Wisdom demands that we give the past its due and get on with the present. Those thoughtful souls who spend years and years in therapy unravelling the yarn from the sweater their parents knitted never get around to designing their own sequined dresses.

There are many metaphysical teachers, who in their certainty that we are responsible for our lives, insist that we pick our own parents. I find that an amazing idea. I have a huge imagination but I can't imagine picking the parents I ended up with! I am certain I would have chosen richer parents if any were available. If I had any say in the matter at all, I would have chosen altogether more advantages.

I was a smart kid and I would have picked people who were more mature, more sensitive, more sensible and above all - wealthier. If I'd had the choices that some people say I did, I'm certain I would have chosen to be born in San Francisco, Paris, Philadelphia or London -

not McAllen, Texas. For that matter, I probably would have chosen to look like Shirley Temple and would have been born in the penthouse of the Plaza Hotel in New York City.

What does seem clear to me is that children come equipped with personalities and arrive, seemingly willy-nilly, in the laps of people who either do or do not want them. That's how we get our "stories" which we carry around until we're ready to let go of them.

We definitely came with unique temperaments which may or may not have been ideally suited to those of our parents. We may even have brought certain complexities of personality or conflicts with us to work out.

As infants, we aren't responsible - we are human infants and that means we simply cannot survive without the help of the elders in the tribe. We didn't invent the world, we didn't earn trouble because of sins in another lifetime and we didn't end up here because Adam ate an apple.

As children, we grow into more and more ability and opportunity to choose. We carry an inner intelligence, which, given any sort of chance at all, will create a guiding light.

As adults, we are more or less responsible for how long we continue to believe we are dependents. We also get to decide how long we carry those "stories" around and what we choose to do when we let go of them.

Preoccupation with the past is usually self-defeating. Don't spend your energy trying to figure out why you picked the parents you did - they were next in line in the butcher shop and your number came up. They wrapped you up, tied a string around you and took you home. From that moment on - you were hamburger. That's enough to know. Now build a good life for yourself!

All children get molded and instructed. Most get sculpted and pummeled a bit. Obviously, adults must impart the accumulated knowledge of their particular culture to children born into that culture. Obviously, some of the knowledge which adults attempt to impart will be unrealistic, out of date and even unpleasant.

One of your first Wisdom Choices is to recognize that the adults in your life probably gave you all they had to give. It may have been cruel, it may have been wrong, it have been harmful but it was <u>what they knew at the time.</u>

Every child goes through some process of enculturation. Parents and teachers speak of it as "civilizing" their little darlings. The little darlings grow up and attempt to march through life with a stiff upper lip, ignoring the pain of not being themselves. Or they join support groups to sort out fact and fiction and discuss their dysfunctional families. Some adopt a new brand of "civilization," moving into radically different lifestyles which can include a change of location, religion and sexual behaviors.

As children, we all get told what to do. Some of what we are told is useful, other parts we discard. Most of us, when we tell our stories, tell them in the form of a kind of mental and spiritual striptease. We speak of old beliefs and how we discarded them, and those of us who see ourselves as more or less free and self-reliant, speak of returning to our original essence.

There is no area of our lives where we need to be more self-reliant and independent than in the area of personal appearance. So many women torture themselves because they do not live up to the image which is presented to them by society.

No one deliberately chooses to make themselves miserable by worrying about appearance, but a lot of us do it unconsciously. If there is something you want to change and you can change it without threatening your life to do it, go ahead and change it. If you can't change it, have the serenity to look beyond the image and find your true beauty which is your natural birthright.

Above all, stick with realistic goals and attitudes. We are besieged by unrealistic standards of beauty. Don't let impossible standards ruin your life. Don't wait until you lose twenty pounds to recognize your essential beauty. Recognize your beauty today! Don't spend your life wishing your hair were curly or your nose were longer or your legs were thinner. Enjoy your unique individualized beauty today!

We really need to monitor this one! To constantly compare ourselves with women who are younger, who are professional beauties or who were given different attributes is an exercise in futility. Watch your conversation when you are with your women friends. Don't allow yourself to slip into hours of "girl talk" about how fat you are or how much you want to change something about your personal appearance.

You want to live a wise and happy existence. You deserve that. Don't let old tapes destroy your present happiness. Don't let the media present unattainable standards. Get on with your life!

It is the return to the essence which is important, not what beliefs we accept or reject. It was the Delphic Oracle who is supposed to have been the first to say that the most important key to wisdom is to "Know Thyself." The advice is good advice.

Most of us who are on Wisdom's Pathway are searching for a way to feel authentic. Before we can do that, we have to be willing to look behind the pleasing photo-exterior and reclaim ourselves. In the search for authenticity, we will find our own unique beauty. That's a promise.

Above all - remember that you must have been a beautiful baby because baby, look at you now!

****

QUESTIONS

1. How beautiful did you feel at age five?

2. Do you believe you know your essential nature? Do you know who you really are?

3. Can you look in the mirror, smile deeply into your own eyes and say, "I love you." Try it - when you get used to it, you'll find it very healing.

AFFIRMATIONS

I am a perfectly beautiful person.

I love life and life loves me.

I love myself the way I am, and I am willing to change.

I love my hair.

I love my skin.

I love my feet.

I love my elbows.

I love my teeth.

I love my scalp.

I love my _____ (fill in the blank.)

CHAPTER
EIGHT

WISE WOMEN DON'T WORRY

It is 1962. Jane is 29 years old. Her daughter has gone to the bottom of Grand Canyon on a mule. Jane is too frightened of heights to have even considered the trip. Jane chose to let her ten-year-old daughter make the trip to the bottom of the canyon with a group of strangers and a guide. Jane's choice is part of an overall choice not to pass on her family fears and phobias to her child.

Now she watches as the mule train descends the steep path. She has already checked the facts out very thoroughly and she knows she has made a rational decision. It doesn't even occur to her that she can control her irrational fears beyond making the decision to let her child go.

She spends eight hours wandering around on the top of Grand Canyon in terror. She can't eat breakfast and only finishes half her lunch. She can't enjoy the day. She turns down her companion's suggestions of alternate activities. Most of the day, she stands at the edge of the canyon, peering down into the terrifying chasm, feeling fear and trembling.

When her companion tells her not to worry, she is furious with him. In her irrational state of mind, worrying seems as though it is her job!

At sundown, the mule train comes up the canyon trail five minutes before the scheduled time. The guide tells her what a great time they all had and what a wonderful daughter she has. Her daughter looks absolutely radiantly happy and wants to go out to see the Indian dancing that evening. Her companion is willing but Jane is too exhausted from all that worry.

****

At the time this incident took place, I seriously would have told you that all good mothers worried. In my delusion, I honestly believed that worry was accomplishing something positive. I believed if a mother worried, she was doing <u>something</u>.

This is a common belief and it contains some level of truth. Worrying is a form of thinking and thinking is doing something. It is sending a message to the Universe. Unfortunately, worrying sends a negative message.

Worry doesn't always bring about the things we worry about. In this case, everything turned out fine. I was exhausted and stiff and miserable but there was no harm beyond that. Random thoughts don't always bring disaster but a consistent pattern of worry can definitely bring trouble.

The confusion around the usefulness and purpose of worry is especially poignant in the area of parenting. How many times have we seen children produce exactly the kind of behavior their parents worried they would? Until we consciously make new choices, we are all in danger of following the life scripts our parents mentally wrote for us. Worry is a very effective form of life-script writing.

Of course, parents of young children have to be protective. To examine the facts and make careful decisions based on rational data is not worry. It is simply using your intelligence. Some parents might not choose to let a ten-year-old take such a journey without them. That's fine. Parents need to make careful decisions and be comfortable with their choices. My decision was based on an overall goal to raise an independent, brave child and it worked for us. It depends a lot on the child and it also depends on the facts. To consider a decision carefully is not negative and it is not worry.

Worry can sometimes cloak a great need to hang on to your children beyond the time to let them take responsibility for their own lives. Parents who lie awake until two in the morning, unable to sleep until their nineteen-year-old son is safely home, always seem proud of the great job they're doing. They tell you they haven't had a wink of sleep and it is clear they take pride in their parenting abilities. What is less clear to them is that their intention to protect and nurture their child is being expressed inappropriately. The fact that the child is nineteen and needs to learn to take care of himself is difficult for them to imagine.

When people begin to consider the ramifications of their past mental activity, it can sometimes bring up questions of guilt or blame. They begin to worry that they used to worry, compounding the interest on the negative thinking until they feel as though they aren't getting much of anywhere with their program of positive thinking.

Trust me - it does no good to worry in the present and it does less good to worry about the past. The past is gone forever and you did the best you could then. The issue in front of you is to do the best you can now!

It is important to recognize that children who are raised by parents who mirror trust and confidence do find their lives are easier. Self-confidence can be given as a gift or earned by the individual. Most of us achieve self-confidence as a result of our own good start in life combined with our own excellent efforts.

If your parents worried a lot when you were a child, you may have picked up the idea that it is now your job to worry for them, for your own children and even for yourself. Again, we assume that worry is a positive activity until we see that there are better ways to think and live.

Worry is not positive. It is negative. It is an attempt on the part of the person doing the worrying to use her God-given intelligence well, but it is actually a misuse of power. Whenever we give ourselves over to worry, we are giving ourselves over to something outside ourselves. Worry is fear and fear is not our highest and best expression of self.

As I walked around in a dazed condition all day long, I intended to accomplish something positive. For me, worrying was a proof of love. I was wrong. The proof of love which I demonstrated was in letting her go down the trail. In retrospect, I define myself as a good parent. I give myself a great deal of credit for cutting the cycle of fear. As for the worry - that was nonsense.

While I think one of the most challenging places to eliminate worry is in the area of parenting, life presents plenty of other opportunities. In the workplace, it is possible to worry yourself half to death about whether or not you will get the promotion you want. Worrying definitely won't help you get that promotion. It may make you pretty miserable in the process, and it could even create a mental atmosphere that is so negative it actually cuts down on your chances. Try daydreaming about getting the job instead of rehearsing what you are going to say when you don't get it. Replace worry with an attitude of expectation.

Worry won't make you prettier either. In fact, worry lines will actually make a beautiful woman ugly. It will show up on your face even if you keep yourself from frowning in public. Your face is a map of your emotional state and people read worry in your eyes, hear it in your voice and sense it in the tension with which you hold your chin. Eliminate worry and be your most beautiful self.

There is no area of your life where worry will actually work in your favor. Despite what your Aunt Leticia may have told you, preparing yourself for the worst does not dampen disappointment, it simply creates disappointment.

Eliminating worry is easier than you might think. The most specific thing you can do for yourself is to practice living one day at a time. If this is difficult, try making a list each morning of the things you want to accomplish that day. Cross them off as you do them and at the end of the day, throw away the list. Tomorrow you can make a new list.

You really can train your mind to focus on the current activity or task. The goal is to stay in the moment. If you are in the park with the kids, don't let your mind wander to tomorrow's meeting. Notice the moment you are in and be happy in that moment. Practice one pointed focus. Smell the air. Hug the kids. Be there totally.

Many women find there are definite activities which set off patterns of worry. If you are in the habit of worrying after you talk on the telephone with Cousin Mabel, think about shortening those telephone calls. If you find the evening news worries you, turn it off and subscribe to a decent newspaper. You have the power to make positive choices in your life. You are in charge.

Some women find that worry is associated with an inability to sleep. You may find it wise to consult an expert on sleep disorders but before you do that, try some of these simple ideas to reduce worry at bedtime.

Try visiting your local health food stores and/or doctor for suggestions about herbal teas, calcium and other supplements which are relaxing and sleep-inducing. You might also try increasing your physical activity during the day so that you will be more relaxed and ready to sleep.

You might consider monitoring the television shows you are watching before bedtime. All that violence and emotional trauma may be more powerful than you suspect. Experiment with comedy shows, classical music and pleasant novels as an alternative to the boxing matches and the eleven o'clock news.

Try using a relaxation tape. There are several good ones on the market and I especially like the ones which include positive affirmations as a part of the relaxation exercises. Write to Cornucopia Press for a catalog of my guided meditations. You can also make your own meditation tape, using suggestions and music which are especially right for you.

Eliminating worry is one of the first and most important steps on Wisdom's Pathway.

****

QUESTIONS

1. Do you see patterns of worry in your current life?

2. What do you want to change?

3. When do you worry, and how might you distract yourself?

AFFIRMATIONS

I live in the present wonderful moment.

I am all right, right here and now.

I love my life and my life is wonderful.

I am worry-free and take perfect right action.

CHAPTER
NINE

WISE WOMEN
CHOOSE MENTORS

It is 1946. Jane is 13 years old. She has heard a man speak at school that day who says he wants to start a teenage group. He says there is a big problem with juvenile delinquency in the United States and his job is to help prevent kids from getting into trouble. He works for an organization called the Community Chest.

Jane is certainly not a juvenile delinquent and she has never heard of the Community Chest but she decides to visit the man after school. He invited anyone who was interested to drop by and she is interested - mostly in knowing more about him.

Most of the kids in her class think the guy is weird. They never met an adult who talks the way he does. He isn't like their teachers or their parents. Jane likes the quiet, intelligent way the man speaks.

She drops by that very afternoon after school. His name is Mr. Myers and he is a tall, gentle man with deep brown eyes and a large nose. She has already heard from the other kids that he is a Jew but she knows nothing of Jews except for photographs in the newspaper of survivors of the Holocaust. This man is an American and fought in World War II so his Jewishness has absolutely no meaning to her at all.

What she likes about him is the way he listens to her and asks questions about what she thinks. By the end of that first afternoon, they have formed a friendship that will last through her high-school years. She will learn a lot from him about how to approach people with respect. She will learn that it is possible to cooperate with people without insisting that there be perfect agreement. She will learn that every person has a central integrity which will respond to respect.

Jane will help him form a club for junior-high students that actually does change lives. She will be president of the club for three years.

The Wilmington Community Center will become a place where kids can come and play pool and talk safely about the things that they really are wondering and worrying about. Mr. Myers will answer questions without telling people what they "ought" to believe. There will be dances every Friday night and many, many trips away from the docks and into the larger world.

Jane will always be Mr. Myers' pet - partly because she is the first to volunteer - mostly because she is eager to learn. From him, she will learn about politics, about modern art, about New York City, about international issues and most of all - she will learn that men don't have to be neurotic, loud or mean. That men can be kind, responsible, caring and effective. That men - as well as women - can make a difference in the quality of people's lives.

****

A mentor is someone who provides a model for a quality or qualities you wish to acquire. It is up to you to choose your mentors. You do not need to take up everyone who offers to provide you with information, inspiration and behavior models.

One of the first hints of how wonderful being an adult is going to be is when we get to the stage where we can actually choose our own mentors. We can seek out adults whom we admire and make it a point to spend time with them. Often, these mentors provide a more balanced view of life than the one we are getting at home. Sometimes these mentors provide an opening onto a larger world.

Mentors are not necessarily friends - they are something like teachers, but you are not a captive in the classroom, you are picking and choosing your own lessons. Mentors are more than substitute parents and their job is more than providing comfort and love. They provide a model for a new vision of greater possibilities, a model to emulate, and information about how to get skills or qualities you admire.

Mr. Myers was the first mentor I chose for myself and my association with him completely changed and enriched my life. To him I owe my absolute conviction that the world is improvable and that I can make a difference.

Choosing a mentor is an act of power for an adult just as it is for a teenager. The choice of mentor depends on what skills you want to acquire. If you want to learn to play the guitar, take some lessons from your local teacher. If you want to be a **great** guitar player and you've already learned all you can from the local talent, find a **great** guitar player and do what you have to to learn from him or her. Hang around, carry coffee, carry the guitar, but make sure you are actually learning something, not just having a great time at the party.

Be honest with yourself when you select someone to lead or guide you. It doesn't matter who the teacher is, you are still in charge of your own learning. Einstein can't teach a kindergartner the theory of relativity and Perlman can't teach you to play the violin if you won't practice. The truth is, it is always up to you to learn. Picking a good mentor can make that job easier - that's all.

Mentors don't have to be of the same gender in order to be effective. In fact, many business and professional women find they are in an environment where they must choose men mentors or have none at all. However, there are possible pitfalls when mentors cross gender lines.

When women choose men as mentors they need to be very clear that they are choosing a mentor, not a father, boyfriend or husband to please. In twelve-step programs, such as Alcoholics Anonymous, it is strongly suggested that you choose a sponsor who is of the same sex and that is for a very good reason. It's not because all men are beasts and all women are birds of prey, it's because our cultural patterning makes it more difficult to keep the relationship simple.

Gender is not the most important quality in choosing a friend, adviser, therapist, coach, director, teacher, or minister (all mentors) to emulate. The most important thing is to be sure that person actually does embody the quality or qualities you are looking to incorporate in your life.

Suppose you have decided to leave your secretarial position and go into business for yourself as a real estate professional. You get your license, hang it in a large office and begin to look around for someone who can help you learn the ropes. You will want to avoid other beginners of course, and you will also want to avoid the agents who grumble and seem to be in lawsuits all the time. In every office there are a few agents who enjoy their work, who are professional and successful, and who know how to work effectively. If you are smart, you will try to get your desk placed next to one of those agents and then you will simply observe.

Observation is a more effective way to learn what people do to be successful than directly asking them questions for two reasons. The first reason is that many people are uncomfortable when they are asked too many direct questions. They carry their own baggage of beliefs which probably include the idea that questions imply criticism. So go easy with the questions - at least at first.

The other reason not to ask questions is more subtle. Most people really aren't clear about how they do what they do well. They do their best work more or less instinctively. They couldn't tell you that as they answer the telephone, they always raise their voices in a joyous expectation. However, you can observe that.

As you observe, you emulate the things you see that might work for you. Make sure you only imitate the positive and appropriate behaviors. If your mentor always wears a red short tight skirt to the Tuesday office meetings, you don't need to imitate her costume, just emulate her promptness and enthusiasm. Leave the leg show to someone else.

As in every area of our lives, we should be willing to give something back in exchange for what we receive. When we are working with a professional who accepts fees, that exchange is fairly straightforward. We pay them money for their time, talent and information. Generally we call the people we pay by names such as coach, director, teacher, or instructor. Never begrudge paying a fair fee and don't try to cut corners. If you get what you want, it is a fair exchange and a good bargain.

When you are selecting a teacher, make sure you have a clear agreement about fees. You can avoid a lot of bruised feelings and unfulfilled expectations if you insist on an actual price at the beginning. Vague deals such as exchanging yard work for writing lessons often lead to real disappointment. Don't let price be your only consideration. Pick the teacher who actually has the most skills to impart.

Once you have signed on for the course, be sure you fulfill your commitment. Guitar lessons won't work if you cancel half the appointments and fail to practice in between. You will simply be paying for a painful hour for you and your teacher. Why pick a writing teacher and pay her good money if you don't want to rewrite?

Mentors are less straightforward and more nearly what we would call, "Life teachers." Often there is no opportunity for direct pay - and it would not be appropriate - but make sure you find ways to give something in return.

It doesn't have to involve a lot of money, but it should be of value to the recipient.

We can't shop for life teachers in the way we shop for a personal fitness trainer. In a way, we are the spiritual student and we must make it our business to be ready so that the teacher can appear.

When I was about 50, I noticed I was beginning to collect friends who were in their 70's and I realized that they were not only friends, they were mentors. The women I picked were women who were aging without losing any of their zest for life, any of their sense of unlimited possibility or their wonderful joy. They were not only friends, they were models for me. They provided a vision of older age which counterbalanced the talk of loneliness, nursing homes, fear and ill health I was hearing all around me.

In order to choose a mentor successfully, you must have a vision about the kind of person you want to be or the skills you want to acquire. Some women spend all their lives going from one dominant teacher to another, modelling themselves after one and then another powerful person without ever discovering the essential core of themselves. This kind of Pygmalian syndrome is not ever going to make a woman happy.

As a young person, it is natural to try out several personalities and even try out following several different kinds of persons, but eventually, we are responsible for our own lives and our own behavioral choices. Make sure when you are choosing a mentor that the person you are choosing is capable of letting you be yourself. If not - march!

In today's world, it is important for older women to offer as much mentoring as they can to the younger ones. Just because we had to more or less invent ourselves doesn't mean that the following generations need to go through the same process. They won't copy us, that's certain, but let us offer as much help as we can.

No one prepared me to be a successful woman. The idea was a kind of oxymoron. I'm ashamed to admit it but I actually was pleased when people told me I had a mind like a man. I was also pleased when I was told I was beautiful and I had a lot of trouble putting the two goals together. Gloria Steinem and the women's movement have done a lot for us all. Let's pass on what we learned where we can.

****

QUESTIONS

1. Do you have women friends who are older than you are?

2. Do you have women friends who are younger than you are?

3. Who have your important mentors been so far? Do you see a pattern?

AFFIRMATIONS

I am my own spiritual teacher.

My perfect mentor now appears in my life.

I am a good mentor for others.

I am willing to learn and be self-reliant at the same time.

CHAPTER
TEN

WISE WOMEN KNOW
HOW TO GET HELP

It is 1969. Jane is 36 years old and her daughter has just gone off to college. It is a Saturday morning and she thinks she will clean the garage. Her dead second husband's junk is in there and it has been cluttering her life for three years. She will take action. She will clean her emotional house and her physical garage. She will make a statement.

Jane believes her life is over and she believes she is very, very depressed. Although she has been able to stay sober on her own for almost ten years, she believes she has a reason to drink. She believes she is tired of teaching, tired of reading, tired of being alone. She believes she is tired of fighting the feelings of hopelessness and despair.

She doesn't really believe that booze will make anything better but she believes she will have a drink anyway. She tells herself that she has decided to face despair and the alcohol will give her the courage to look at her deepest feelings. She goes to the liquor store and buys some wine and after nine years of sobriety, she begins to drink again.

It is, in its way, a conscious decision but it feels as though some hidden part of Jane is making the choice. She is on "automatic pilot" as she drives to the grocery store and comes home with a jug of Gallo red.

As she drinks wine, she plays her blues records and dances. She dances alone, banging against tables, finally slipping and falling before she passes out. She vomits of course. That seems appropriate. She believes she is sick of life. She believes she is afraid and alone. She believes she is living the blues. And she believes she is being honest.

She sees herself as a sort of aging Janis Joplin who can't sing. She identifies totally with her dear dead friend, Billie Holiday. She loves the blues and the blues serve her by carrying her to the level where she has planned to sink. The wine and the blues serve her purpose to self-destruct.

****

In this Age of Recovery, my story will be recognized as one variation on the many reasons which women give for addictive behavior. I have come to understand that the unplumbed depths of despair which caused me to drink also caused me to smoke, chase unacceptable men, shop too much, and eat too much. These days, the feelings are much more recognizable and the behavior only surfaces from time to time in shopping and eating. I have the wisdom to know that's progress!

But things were very different in 1969. I was very frightened and ashamed of my behavior. I was living in the suburbs, surrounded by tract houses which I honestly believed were stuffed full of "normal" people.

The only people I knew who drank the way I drank were in Russian novels. Nowhere else could I find that peculiar blend of emotionalism, romanticism, despair and alienation which crept out of hiding when I was drinking. I simply did not understand the person who drank and yet I knew she represented a part of me which could actually kill me.

It is no accident that women suffer from so many addictive diseases. Some are alcoholics or drug addicts. Many others are involved in eating disorders. Compulsive shoppers and gamblers live lives of financial failure while people who are compulsive in their sexuality are creating their own personal hells.

The underlying causes for compulsive behavior in women are pretty apparent. When one is required to blind oneself to so much of what is going on, the result is blindness.

Even after our eyes are open and we are able to see that our behavior is out of control, there can be such a strong sense of helplessness and hopelessness that nothing is done. And women suffering from addictions feel so unacceptable and alone!

Addiction is a tricky issue to deal with because it strikes at the heart of the problem of repression versus expression. This is an issue which affects all women - even those who do not have addictive personalities.

How and why should I express my whole personality if parts of that personality are negative, frightening and apt to kill me? How do I draw the line between normal and out of control? What can I do if I am out of control?

It is crucial to stop the addictive behavior as completely as you can. It is also crucial to acknowledge the fear, rage, despair and other negative feelings which create the behavior. These feelings can be known and dealt with instead of being submerged torpedoes which suddenly sink the ship.

Twelve Step groups are statistically the most effective way to overcome addictive behavior. I believe that is because of the wonderful step program which is based on spiritual principles. It is also true that twelve-step programs are effective because they are so available. In most areas of the United States and Canada, one can find meetings at any time of day or night. One can find fellow humans who will listen and understand. One need never be alone with the problem again. Twelve-step programs break the cycle of secrecy and alienation and they are free, abundant and spiritually sound.

Psychological counseling is as good as the individual counselor so choose carefully if you go that route. I believe you should make sure you find someone with more than textbook familiarity with addiction. I always recommend women counselors for women and I would want to know that the therapist supports twelve-step philosophy.

Prayer or spiritual mind treatment is a powerful force for good and I recommend it as an adjunct to the twelve-step programs. Make sure your pastor understands addiction as a disease and is not into condemning you for your behavior. Only a supportive environment will work well.

One final important point - your goal should be to stop the behavior and defuse or eliminate the negative emotions which caused it. Don't fall into the trap of thinking you can eliminate emotions so well that you can reinstate "normal" behavior. There is a good chance that you never really had a "normal" to reinstate, and so that idea is a blueprint for disaster. Only an insane person would want to risk it again. I'm real clear on that point and I hope you are as well.

****

QUESTIONS

1. Does any of your past behavior seem addictive?

2. Do you think you might have a problem with alcohol or drugs?

3. Do you think you might have an eating disorder?

4. Do you have skills for coping with negative emotions?

AFFIRMATIONS

I am a worthwhile person.

My life is a good life right now.

I love my life and I express all my best ideas.

I look forward to each day.

CHAPTER
ELEVEN

WISE WOMEN
BECOME THEMSELVES

It is 1961. Jane is 28 years old. She is giving a workshop at an all day teacher training. She is one of many classroom teachers who have been selected throughout the district to share special skills. She wanted to turn down the opportunity down but didn't know how to say no without damaging her rating in the district. She has not spoken in public since she was fifteen.

Her workshop is on teaching poetry to junior high students. She is comfortable taking part in class discussions but she cannot imagine enjoying the opportunity to stand in front of an audience.

She is anxious for several days before the event and plans her workshop carefully. Once there, she is nervous about being in front of her peers, however she is well prepared and quickly begins reading the poems her students have written. In between their poems, she talks about the activities and exercises she's used to stimulate their writing. Soon, she is quite comfortable and simply teaching school to a different group of students. Things are going well.

About fifteen minutes into her hour-and-a-half program, the superintendent of schools walks in. Though she has never met him, she recognizes him immediately. He is greatly feared throughout the school district because he is an opinionated, outspoken and rude man. Tales from the principal's meetings sound like nightmares of verbal abuse although he seldom meddles in local school business.

All her fear of authority races in to numb her out. She feels dizzy and wants to run. She thinks she may even faint! Her knees begin to cave in so she leans against the desk. Jane's voice begins to tremble, but she continues to read, telling herself she must simply continue with her program and he will soon be gone. Her only other option is to run away and that doesn't seem possible.

The superintendent continues to sit and listen. She goes on with her workshop, talking to some place slightly over his head and to the left. He spends a whole hour in her room and then stalks out just before the workshop is over.

She is shattered and nervous the rest of the day but by evening, she decides it will not make or break her life. At least she got through the ordeal and she can call that progress.

One week later, her principal calls her in to the office and thanks her for doing such a fine job. He says the superintendent spent quite a bit of time at the principal's meeting talking about how successful the day was and especially, how great her workshop was. All is well.

****

We are always in the process of growing and changing and of becoming more and more our true selves. Often, our decision to express a more competent, more successful, more alive self requires the courage to face negative emotions and go through some real changes.

There is an old joke in which two women meet on the street and one says to the other, "I'm going through Hell."

The second woman says, "Keep on moving."

We need to be willing to keep moving in our own lives even when what we are going through is very difficult. To back down and let fear rule is to be faced with another choice and another challenge the next day. Life is not a horse and we don't always have to get back on and ride again, but if fear is curtailing our life choices, we should think about saddling up.

Our current situations in life are more or less a result of a series of choices we have made up to now. We can make new choices, but first we need to acknowledge how fear has kept us from making the choices we wanted to in the past. Then we have to be willing to walk through the fear.

Shelters for battered women are filled by women who haven't yet found the courage to go through the fear they face when they think of leaving a relationship. Incredible as it may seem to someone who has lived on her own, many wonderful women stay in really terrible situations because they are afraid of being alone.

The few real recluses I have known in my life have become isolated and housebound through a series of choices made over a period of years. Each time they turned down an invitation, they put another nail in the coffin they were building around themselves.

Overcoming anything that limits our successful lives, whether it is stage fright, fear of authority, fear of speaking out, or fear of flying means going through the old emotions and choosing to replace fear, anger or some other negative emotion with the love of life and self-love. A strong spiritual connection and an understanding that God supports any activity which is life-affirming can really speed up the process of change.

We are all so wonderful! Within our natural essence there is such promise and such an unlimited range of possibilities. Learning to be the very best Jane or Mary or Natasha or Glenda is really worth the trouble and possible pain.

I know a woman who decided she wanted to have a healthy old age. Despite the fact that she was 50 and had never exercised in her life, she undertook the study of yoga. Each time she made the choice to attend yoga class, she was choosing a greater expression of her own potential. Although it is easy to put classes in a secondary position, she made them a priority. She was older than the other yoga students and she was a busy grandmother with many interests. Nevertheless, she went to yoga week after week for ten years. By the time she was sixty she not only had a beautiful, flexible body but she could do a full headstand and some other difficult postures which many younger people never achieve.

Expressing your potential is wonderful work. Not expressing your potential creates dis-ease, unhappiness and even tragic lives. Many people who experience ill health find that expressing their creative talents really helps them heal.

Failure at age fifteen is no reason to quit trying. In my case, it would have surely been tragic since I have come to believe I am in this life to be a teacher. What good is a teacher who cannot speak out? On the other hand, a teacher who has progressed through dumbness to speaking up is especially valuable because she understands the power of fear and she also understands that it is possible to harness the emotion and go on with life.

Dealing with blocked potential is often the way to true happiness though it does require the courage to change. I see so many women who would be talented musicians or talented writers if they were willing to pay the price of moving through the emotional blocks which are standing in their way. Most procrastination is disguised fear. So is most perfectionism. Believe it or not, we invite most of the obstacles we find in our pathway to success.

****

QUESTIONS

1. Have you ever let fear block your expression?

2. If you were to tap into your unlimited potential in a new way, what might that look like?

3. Select a situation you'd like to change in your life. Do you see how a pattern of small choices might eventually create the change you seek? Where might you begin?

4. Do you have special talents you'd like to express more?

AFFIRMATIONS

I let my light shine brightly.

I am a powerful woman.

I move through life, full speed ahead.

Nothing stops me or slows me down.

I am on course!

CHAPTER
TWELVE

WISE WOMEN
RECOGNIZE WINDOWS

It is 1941. Jane is nine years old. She is sitting on a window seat in yet another new house. This one has two fat palm trees in the front yard and a bedroom for her and her sister. It also has a window seat in the dining room where Jane can sit and read in quiet. In the afternoon, the light streams through dark, divided window panes and makes patterns on the floor.

A visitor comes through the window, riding the light as though it were a slide in the park. The visitor talks to Jane for quite a while, telling her things that she will not remember about her past and then the visitor tells her, "You can be anything you want to be, you know. You can do anything you want to do."

Jane listens quietly, not sure if anything is required of her. The visitor seems to be made of the same light that it rides. Jane isn't sure whether it is a man or woman but the voice does not frighten her. The voice sounds exactly like her own voice only it is coming from a visitor outside of herself who travels through glass on light waves. "Study very hard," the visitor says, "You are specially chosen to teach."

The light fades and so does the visitor. Jane goes back to her book, imagining that the event never happened. It is filed, along with many other earlier events in the box in Jane's brain which is labeled, "Do Not Open."

****

Learning to listen to your inner voice is difficult at first, especially if you are the sort of person who was dissuaded from relying on her intuition when she was a child.

All children have natural conversations with their inner voices and many even have imaginary companions. Some apparently have the ability to see things that adults cannot. Not too long ago I was at an outdoor picnic and a four-year-old pointed to the sky just above the picnic table and said, "There's grandpa."

This child's great grandfather had made his transition just a week before. We adults saw nothing and simply looked at each other across the table. The child then lowered his hand and stopped pointing and said, "That's right. Grown-ups don't see ghosts."

It is not the business of this book to argue whether or not there really was something there but I am happy to report that none of us told the child that the vision was "crazy."

When I was a child, I was told I was crazy so often, that for years I refused to hear the promptings of my own inner mind. I simply didn't trust myself to know what I knew. Not being able to listen to your own inner voice leads to a sense of desolation and dependency. When we believe we cannot trust ourselves, we are at a loss as to how to proceed in the world.

As most mystics will tell you, turning within leads to a new kind of guidance and it also leads to some wonderful <u>direct knowings.</u> If I had continued to refuse to know myself, as I tried to do, I would have missed many rich experiences. I would also have missed the path to genuine happiness.

Genuine happiness has to be based on knowing yourself and understanding your deepest dreams and desires. As long as we are completely directed outward, we feel unauthentic and distressed.

During the last twenty years of my spiritual studies I have come to the conclusion that I was very psychic as a child and that I saw many things which other people were unable to see. When I mentioned anything that would be considered to be from <u>another reality</u> it was greeted with fear and I was quickly told I was crazy.

As I have opened up to who I really am, I have come to understand that I see differently than many people. I see intuitively and that's not crazy - it's simply my unique way of viewing the universe.

My intuition has made me a master teacher. As a pastor, it has helped me surround myself with wonderful women and men who are truly loving and supportive. It was a great help in the real estate business. More and more, I have come to depend on my inner guidance to lead me to the path which will be best, be easiest or be most rewarding.

Intuition whispers for everyone. With attention and trust, you can get more than whispers out of that inner guidance. You can pick and choose your friends. You can pick and choose your activities. You can even pick and choose your restaurants by following your intuition.

The intuitive mind is really just a part of your own mind which doesn't have the same limits around it. We are all connected to the Universal Mind and our limits are there because we agree that they should be there. If we are willing to expand the limits, we can do so.

How do we expand our mental limits without being foolish? Meditation is the key. Working with your creative imagination and beginning to follow your hunches is a beginning. As you progress in your ability to <u>know</u> without having the usual data, you will find it becomes easier and easier. And you can validate your results through observation.

Spiritual studies, most especially meditation and learning to listen with a receptive mind, will definitely bring increased promptings of the intuition. Women have traditionally been more open to inner worlds and I believe it is for this reason that they have often been natural healers.

Develop your intuition! Your hunches can make you rich. They can keep you safe. They can lead you to a world of wonder and delight. They can bring you to a place in consciousness where you don't make mistakes about people. Most of all, your intuition can lead you to your true identity and your true purpose in life.

****

QUESTIONS

1. Do you rely on intuition?

2. Do you ever have ideas, thoughts or dreams which seem to come from outside yourself?

3. Do you trust your own instincts?

AFFIRMATIONS

I trust my inner guidance.

I trust myself to do what is best.

I am guided and supported in every aspect of my life.

CHAPTER
THIRTEEN

WISE WOMEN ARE ASSERTIVE

It is 1948 and Jane is 15 years old. She is working in the fanciest dress shop in Redondo Beach as a part-time salesperson. She has lied about her age and she has also lied about where she goes to school. Her boss has already figured out both lies but he likes her. She is a good salesperson.

It is early Friday evening and the store is empty. A black woman and two men come into the store and begin looking through the expensive suits. The sales women huddle around the cash register and her boss whispers, "Just ignore them. We don't want them to try anything on."

Jane says, "I don't think that's right." She moves out from behind the cash register and goes over to the three people. She shows the woman clothes and the woman tries on three expensive suits. She buys the most *expensive one - a gray wool with a peplum and black collar and big cuffs. Jane rings up the $110 sale and takes the woman's cash. It is the best sale of the week.*

After the three people leave, her boss says, "From now on when any colored people come in, let the kid wait on them. She knows how to talk to them."

****

Opportunities to help yourself and others break out of false patterns of belief are presented on a daily basis. Women approach these opportunities with a variety of attitudes, but it is safe to say that women generally have a hard time defying authority or breaking with established custom. Some of us really need to learn to be more assertive.

Sometimes we find it easier to defend others than it is to stand up for our own rights. A lot of women have an especially difficult time getting into open conflict with someone we love. It's as if we find disagreement the exact opposite of love. Yet we all know it is very possible to disagree with someone we love. We know that but what we don't know is that it is all right to disagree out loud.

There have been many books, tapes and workshops available on assertiveness and assertiveness training in the past twenty years. Most of those have been aimed specifically at women. The main point is to persist in stating your objections without giving up, getting into anger or breaking into tears.

We need not be too hard on ourselves for having such a difficult time with speaking up. When you realize most little girls are taught from the day they are born that their value is found in their ability to please others, you can see that it can be very scary to say, "No. I don't agree with that and I'm not going to do it."

We are trained to be pleasing and go along with the program, but it doesn't always work well for us, nor does it always work well for the human race. Think of the effective ways in which women who haven't gone along with the program have been able to change things. See the new legislation on day care, on early childhood education, on family leave and on part-time benefits.

The peace movement was fueled by women who wouldn't go along with the Cold War for many, many years. In the last few years we have seen the collapse of the Berlin Wall, the end of the Cold War, and some other wonderful signs of a new consciousness dawning. I believe that the real power behind all those political reforms has come from groups all over this nation organizing to speak out for peace and also by the many church groups which end their services each Sunday by singing the Peace Song.

Change happens when we can envision it and speak out. For that reason, assertiveness is a very valuable commodity among the peace-loving women of the world. It is also a very valuable commodity when it comes to arranging your world the way you want. If you are not willing to at least say what you want, how can you expect anyone to give it to you?

Create a vision of the world you want. State that vision clearly and speak out whenever you can for that vision. Take the steps that seem sensible and never, never give up.

Modern life is demanding a new level of assertiveness in women and we are perfectly capable of responding. The way we approach challenges may be different, but it can be very, very effective. Persistence does win the day.

As women come to understand their true power and their true worth, they will be much better at taking care of themselves and their children. To continue to let half the children in the United States live in families below the poverty line is unthinkable. We can and will certainly speak up for the children!

In recent years, there has been an attempt to force men to pay the back child support they owe, but the sad truth is that only about half of the single female parents ever get a dollar from their ex-husbands for the welfare of their children. Assertiveness could create a better way.

****

QUESTIONS

1. On an assertiveness scale of 1 to 10 where would you say you were?

2. How would you like to change that?

3. Tell about one time when you were effective in pursuing a goal through your assertiveness skills.

AFFIRMATIONS

I love myself and I take good care of myself.

I am very clear and persistent.

I can state my views without getting upset or angry.

CHAPTER
FOURTEEN

WISE WOMEN CAN
CHANGE THEIR MINDS

It is 1968. Jane is thirty-five years old. She is working part time for the California Teacher's Association, the Torrance Teacher's Association and the Lawndale Teacher's Association. She organizes the Lawndale teachers in the first teacher's strike in California. It is a two day walk out and they get what they want.

Jane applies for 27 openings all over the nation for positions with teachers' associations. Though she is well qualified, she is not asked to come for even one interview. There are no women doing this work and no others have even applied. Jane is offered another year of part-time work for low pay.

She has begun writing and she realizes she is beginning to lose interest in organizational work. She wants more time for reading, literature and poetry. She drops out of organizational work, starts teaching in a new district, and begins to write seriously.

The next year, she receives a call from a colleague who wants her to go to work helping the Los Angeles teachers in their first strike. She says no, she is writing now. The colleague is angry and accuses her of giving up on her dream. When she assures him this is not true, that she has simply found a deeper interest, he asks how she can abandon their worthwhile cause. He says he doesn't understand how she can put her private concerns above the needs of the group. She feels guilty but doesn't give in.

Later, when she thinks about it, she reminds herself that this colleague and the others didn't want her when she was available. Even as she tries to counter her guilt with anger, she knows she simply has changed her mind. Nevertheless, it is easier for her to think of herself as a victim than to simply say, "I've decided to put myself first. I want something different."

****

One fear that keeps women from setting clear-cut goals is the idea that if we set our goals, we will be stuck with them forever. Once we acknowledge that we have the power to go after whatever we want, we soon ask, "But what if I don't like it?"

The answer is, "You can change your mind."

There is great freedom in acknowledging your God-given ability to change your mind. Many of us grew up with a saying, "You made your bed, now lie in it." but we also grew up with another saying, "Take up your bed and walk." The second saying involves healing and when we are healed, we do know that it is possible to change our minds without causing the sky to fall.

There are very few enterprises which require absolute commitment. Certainly someone who goes through twelve years to be a brain surgeon will feel committed to give it a real try, but I actually know a brain surgeon who finished school and decided to become an actor.

I personally believe that child-rearing is a real commitment - one that should be entered into with care, and once entered into, should be completed lovingly. To abandon a child emotionally or physically is cruel. Nor would I be willing to totally abandon an aging parent or spouse, though I would certainly arrange my life so that it was a life, not just a caretaking chore.

Other than brain surgery and the obvious commitments to loved ones, you can change your mind about anything at all. You can be a Democrat and become a Republican. You can live in the Mid-West and move to Florida. You can be a car salesperson and become a painter. You can be a painter and switch to social work.

It is not world threatening to make a new decision. You can change your mind and the globe keeps on turning. Sticking with things you've outgrown or decided you don't like is just another version of being in the "clean plate club." It leads to dis-ease, lethargy and unhappiness. You don't have to finish those lumpy potatoes and you don't have to work at something you hate. You do have freedom to choose.

Once I got hold of the idea that God was not an angry old man in the sky, but a constantly creating process of life, I began to see my life as full of opportunity.

Once I stopped looking at the obstacles and started looking at the opportunity, I was filled with joy and excitement. Imagine a life in which you can think whatever you want, be just about whatever you want, and do nearly anything you want.

Just suppose for a minute that you really believed that. How does it feel? That is a freedom which frightens some because they don't understand their real position in life. We are all on the edge of unlimited opportunity. I love the image of standing on the lip of time - either at dawn, dusk or high noon - but always just at the edge of opportunity and being able to step off into any direction.

Suppose you are working in a store and you think you'd really like to be a travel agent. You think you would like working with people, helping them plan their trips and you hear you can make great money in the travel business. Besides, you love to travel and you think you'd like the perks.

You go to school at night and take the accredited courses. Then you take a part-time job in the travel agency on Saturdays and Sunday afternoons just to see if you really like it. You may even quit your job in the store and try it full time.

After a while, you may discover that you really dislike the complicated computer work and find that flying on short trips to Timbucktoo is hard work. You may decide to go back to the store or you may try real estate sales. Your mother-in-law may think you wasted time and money and energy on the travel business but she is wrong. You now have the information you needed and you're ready to go on with your life.

Changing one's mind is very difficult for some people and too easy for others. There is a middle ground which we can strive for. If you find yourself constantly moving from occupation to occupation or boyfriend to boyfriend, that is a call for a different kind of action. You need to develop middle-ground courage that will enable you to stick with something long enough to really give it a chance. The chapter on persistence is written especially for you.

Most women identify with words such as faithful, persevering, responsible, and reliable and we are inclined to stay too long, do too much and change too slowly. Risk taking is for our faster sisters, we stay in the same town, in the same job, with the same struggles in our marriage until time creates something new in our lives. The idea of breaking away is entertaining and we love movies like *Alice Doesn't Live Here Anymore* but we can't even bring ourselves to change our hairstyle or our favorite colors.

Look in your high-school yearbook and now look in the mirror. Have you changed your makeup? Your hair? Your weight? Your smile? Now look in your closet. Are most of your clothes one color? Two colors? Is blue really your favorite color or do you just wear it because your mother said you had pretty blue eyes? Do you wear your hair short because you like it or because you were taught that women over thirty five shouldn't wear their hair below their shoulders? Do you like the way you look or do you secretly dream of a different wardrobe and appearance?

You may have been a blonde all your life, but you can change your mind and be a red head. You may have lived in the country all your life, but you can move to the city. You may have washed and ironed your blouses all your life, but you can send them to the cleaners. Little choices add up to a different lifestyle. Little choices add up to freedom.

Big choices are possible for women who understand they have the power to be themselves and that they are supported in their choice to be themselves by life itself. When we have developed the inner resources, we can choose to take risks or we can choose to stay with what we are doing. It's not really that one choice is better than another - the beauty is in knowing that you do have choices and you are making them.

****

QUESTIONS

1. What have I changed my mind about in the past?

2. What would I like to change my mind about right now?

3. What do I think of my ability to make choices right now? Do I feel free?

4. What needs to change in order for me to feel free?

AFFIRMATIONS

I am making positive choices in my life right now.

I am supported by Life itself and I can change many things if I want to change them.

I am a powerful woman who makes powerful choices.

I love myself and I love my strength and power.

CHAPTER
FIFTEEN

WISE WOMEN ARE SERENE

It is 1978. Jane is 45 years old. She is meditating in her own home - sitting quietly and following her breath, as she has been doing nearly every morning for the past two years. She is counting her exhalations from 1 to 10 and then starting over again.

As she counts, she receives a gift from the Universe. She sees herself - really sees images of herself in physical form - as though she were reviewing her life before death. She sees herself at age 3, age 12, age 27, age 35 and again at age 43. In each of these sightings, she is doing something ordinary, such as walking home from school or ironing a dress, and in every instance she is radiantly beautiful. It is like looking at a movie except much more because the person she sees is exquisite - a radiant being of light - moving through life with serenity and grace.

She accepts the images as truth and continues counting her breath, but she knows she will see herself differently from now on. She now knows the words, perfect, whole and complete, apply to her.

****

Inner serenity comes from accepting the things you cannot change, changing the things you can and having the wisdom to know the difference. It also comes from intentional thinking and concentrated focus on who and what you wish to become.

Anyone can achieve more serenity and a greater sense of harmony of life through the practice of meditation. There is nothing mysterious or difficult about sitting still for twenty minutes a day and focusing your whole attention on your breath. In the focus, one quiets the mind and achieves a new balance with life.

It is possible to teach yourself meditation through reading a book or through simply sitting. It is not necessary to go to an ashram, nor is it necessary to spend a lot of money for special mantras, incantations or charms. Everything you need to know is already inside yourself, just waiting for a chance to teach you. You are always your own best teacher though others may point out the way.

Although my example of seeing myself was wonderful for me, it is not the goal of meditation to have a special experience. The goal is to quiet the mind, not necessarily to have any sort of experience at all. It is simply enough to be present and quiet for a short time each day. That in itself is so healing and so life-shaping that it can change everything.

Recently, there was a movie about the life of the singer Tina Turner. While the movie was distressing because of the emotional and physical violence which is displayed, it is one of the best sales pitches for meditation I have ever seen. In *What's Love Got To Do With It*, the turning point in Tina Turner's life hinges on her choice to become someone who meditates frequently. Though we are not certain how long it takes her to make the necessary changes, we see the direct connection between her decision to go within and her decision to claim a better life for herself.

It is easy to get caught up in the surface activity of life and much of our confusion, disappointment and unrest comes from the way we swim in shallow water and allow the waves of everyday events to buffet us about.

Each time we choose to sit in meditation, we are choosing to do something for ourselves which is life-affirming, life-changing and life-enhancing. While one twenty minute session won't appear to accomplish much, a year or two of daily meditations will change your whole world.

What actually happens when you meditate? I believe the simplest way to explain it is to say that you detach from the surface activity of life and go into a space which is nearer your inner silence. On a purely physical level, we are told that it changes our brain wave patterns and has certain beneficial effects such as lowering blood pressure. In eastern spiritual traditions, that silence we find in meditation is sometimes called the ultimate reality and sometimes called nothingness.

I believe that inner silence is the fastest way to contact your link to Divine Intelligence - it is the way of your divinity. Ultimately, meditation is a practice, not an abstraction which can be explained.

There are many different names for what I am talking about. In metaphysics, we sometimes call it that still small voice within. Ancient Judaism spoke of the Divine Spark and claimed that it was in all life. The Master Teacher Jesus was giving an instruction in getting silent when he said we should go into our closet to pray.

Whether through meditation or simply through taking long walks or swimming laps each day in a quiet pool, you will benefit from some silent time. We are besieged with noise and we are rushed beyond the wildest dreams of our grandmothers.

In those olden days when most people lived on the farm, life had a natural rhythm tied to the cycles of nature. The summers were busy but the winters provided long hours of quiet and solitude. Whether we know it or not, we miss that quiet time. It is in the quiet time that we make contact with our own inner strength. It is also in the quiet time that we make contact with our Ultimate Source.

In some ways, meditation is a part of a pattern which can become a positive circle. This whole book is aimed at showing you that you have the power to create a wonderful life for yourself by making wonderful choices. Before you are really going to be willing to make those choices, you are going to need to love yourself enough to know that you deserve the best. If you love yourself enough, you will carve a place in your busy day for some quiet, solitary time in which you can simply be you. That meditation time will reinforce your ability to love yourself which will reinforce your ability to make more positive choices.

****

QUESTIONS

1. Do you meditate currently?

2. If you were going to choose to meditate, where would you put that twenty minutes into your schedule?

3. Are there other quiet activities which you enjoy currently? (They might include swimming, walking, listening to classical music, painting or simply lying in the sun.)

AFFIRMATIONS

I have plenty of quiet time.

I am perfect, whole and complete right now.

I am centered in peace and truth.

I am well balanced, and perfectly poised on this planet.

I am filled with joy and a sense of well-being.

CHAPTER
SIXTEEN

WISE WOMEN KNOW GLASS
CEILINGS ARE PLASTIC

It is 1961. Jane is 28 years old. She is having a talk with her daughter, who is 9, about the girl's future career plans. She likes to chat with her child about the future, gently guiding her in the direction of a college education and possibly a Ph.D.

Her daughter says, "I think I'll be a minister when I grow up."

Jane laughs and says, "There aren't women ministers. You'd better think of something else."

"Well what can I be?" her daughter sounds a bit annoyed. She has already learned she's not going to make it onto the fire department staff and astronauts are also out.

"You could be a teacher," Jane says. "Or you might like to be a lawyer. How would you like to teach in a college?"

"I'll think about it," her daughter says.

(postscript...The child actually grows up to be a farmer for ten years, then goes into the construction business, and then gets an MBA in business! And Mama becomes a minister.)

****

Startling changes in opportunity were taking place in the 1960s and 1970s and they continue to revolutionize the workplace today. Women have flooded the fields of real estate and are moving into the ministry in large numbers. There are women in fire and police departments, in medicine, in the military, in law offices and corporation executive suites, and even a few in spaceships.

Despite the amazing changes, most women continue to work in traditional female jobs and continue to earn less than their male colleagues. Those who chose non-traditional pathways have broken ground and have encountered difficulties getting to the top of the organizational ladder. We speak of "the glass ceiling" which serves as an invisible barrier and, of course, there is some truth to the idea that it is difficult for men to give up their places around the boardroom table.

There isn't always a lot we can do about that. However, there is another side to the story that we do have control over. We can control how we view ourselves. We can switch from the idea that we are victims to the idea that we are winners with much to offer the boys in the boardroom.

As women, we have become accustomed to thinking of ourselves as powerless. As political women, we are in the habit of noticing every slight and every piece of evidence that reinforces our victim role.

In the workplace and at home, we need to claim and keep our power and act as independently as we possibly can. There is no gain in sulking, whining or getting mad and refusing to play the game. We carry a lot of the little girl waiting to dance around with us every day. We can't let that little girl ruin our lives, you know.

Have you noticed how many women buy into the idea that their lives are miserable because some man wouldn't give them what they wanted? That is nonsense. If men were capable of giving women what they wanted, they would have done so by now - even if it meant sharing the key to the executive washroom.

Everyone knows there is a glass ceiling, the important news is that we are all keeping it in place. The glass ceiling is actually more than a ceiling. It is like a huge fishbowl of custom and belief.

We sometimes call this fishbowl our culture, sometimes we call it Western civilization, and sometimes we can't see it well enough to call it anything. We just say, "This is the way we do things."

For most of us, the fishbowl is large enough that we are happy swimming around, living - and sometimes even enjoying - our lives. We learn early how to avoid bumping our noses. We develop habits, patterns and lifestyles which allow us to forget about or simply not see the curtain of custom which cuts off our freedom.

The problem is that the curtain of custom is so transparent that can you bump into it. Bumping into it can be painful and sometimes dangerous, but if you look at history, you will discover that the glass ceiling, the cultural fishbowl, and the curtain of custom are made out of a material more like soft plastic than glass.

Plastic doesn't shatter, it yields when enough force is applied. It is not glass at all. If you swim through it, you will simply be on the outside looking in. If enough of us bump into the curtain, custom itself will change shape.

What we are looking for is a critical mass of Wise Women who can push out the boundaries of our cultural norms without creating painful conflict, but by gently and not-so-gently extending the limits.

It is the little choices which work miracles. Every time you choose to speak up and say what you think, you add to the general belief that women have something valuable to say. Every time a woman works actively in a political campaign or runs for local school board, the political clout of women is taken more seriously. Every time a woman is considered for a promotion and gets it without reference to her gender, we are all empowered.

Complaining about the past doesn't work. Neither does direct confrontation in most cases. Assuming that every man you meet is the enemy is just plain foolish. For Wise Women, generalities just don't work. Specific instances of kindness, of creativeness, of consideration and of courage should be recognized and encouraged.

Computer models which say women won't gain parity in the work place for three hundred years are nonsense! They base their projections on past performance, not on the power of positive thinking. Wise Women know that positive thinking can change things quickly and there is a whole lot of positive thinking going on right here and now.

There is no such thing as a glass ceiling. There is no such thing as a general conspiracy to keep women in low-paying jobs. There is a whole lot of rethinking which we need to do. Let us revise our attitudes and watch it happen.

****

QUESTIONS

1. What is it like for you at your workplace?

2. How would you like to see it change?

3. What belief about yourself would you have to change to make a difference in the workplace?

4. When you speak up, are you heard?

5. How would you like to be heard? Can you ask for that?

AFFIRMATIONS

I love my work and I am well paid and well treated.

I love myself and my work.

I am a wonderful person and a wonderful worker.

My work day goes smoothly and everything is accomplished easily.

My wonderful work is recognized and well paid.

I am a competent worker in pleasant surroundings.

CHAPTER
SEVENTEEN

WISE WOMEN
CAN TOUCH SOURCE

It is 1976. Jane is 43 years old. She is living in Mexico, writing books that don't sell and drinking too much. For the last six weeks she has been sober and she feels slightly hopeful. It is a fragile sobriety, but six weeks is a little bit of time. She hopes she may make it.

She has been involved with a married man - an older American who winters in Mexico - for three years, and against her better judgment, she has gone away for a week in Puerto Angel with him and his wife. Drinking, she rather enjoyed a starring role in this particular soap opera. Sober, it doesn't really fit her values, but since she believes she is in love, she wants to please him.

She plays along with the game. The game is that his wife doesn't know about them. It is a bad, bad week and Jane has managed to stay sober. Now they are going home.

He and his wife have quarreled all week. The three of them are now driving back from Puerto Angel to Oaxaca, Mexico. The road is steep, dangerous and there are portions where the road has actually just fallen away from the hillside. The drop is a half mile-sheer.

His wife is drinking and she suddenly flies into a wild rage and begins to scream. Jane goes numb, not so much from fear, but from the appalling rage which is circling around the car. At one point, his wife actually grabs the wheel of the car and tries to run them off the road.

The best way to describe her behavior is to picture Jung's anima on a whirlwind of vengeance. Rage, red, and violence fill the car.

Jane's lover says nothing. His hands grip the steering wheel very tightly and he pushes his wife away twice when she grabs the steering wheel and tries to hit him. It is entirely possible that she will cause all three to die but he just keeps driving, pretending it isn't happening.

Jane sits quietly, wishing with all her heart that she were somewhere else. Jane hates scenes and this is the worst scene she's ever been a part of in her whole life. She is too numb to feel much, but she knows that fear and guilt are rolled up into an emotional nightmare.

No one seems particularly worried about falling off the edge of the earth. The violence of the private drama is too gripping. He drives and grimly refuses to respond. She screams and screams, shouting obscenities and dragging up real and false wounds. Jane is paralyzed into complete silence and feeling that she is in so much pain that it would be all right to go over the edge.

It is as though the whole car is choked with emotion and none of it is honest. The wife's tirade is horrible but fake because she never directly says she thinks he and Jane are having an affair. His silence is as angry as her shouting and just as poisonous.

Jane feels guilty and denies it, refusing to recognize her self-hatred and projecting it onto the wife. She sees herself - not as the "other woman" but as victim - and the wife as a witch. She represses her own anger at her lover for not leaving his wife long ago. Jane doesn't realize it, but she feels as she felt as a small child when bad things happened. She cannot remember those events, but she remembers how to get very, very quiet and hope she won't be noticed as the battles rage.

They stop in a small mountain town for gas and Jane gets out of the car. She is more or less in shock from trying to deal or rather - not deal - with all the negative energy blasting around inside that vehicle. Her panic is great enough that all she wants is to escape. She insists they leave her there, that she will hitch a ride home with some passing strangers.

They are all three familiar enough with Mexico to know that would be an extremely dangerous thing to do. He would never be that irresponsible and he is so numbed by ersatz emotion that he probably thinks Jane is bluffing. But Jane is not bluffing, she is at the end of her ability to tolerate the scene and flight is the only solution she has ever known.

Jane is ready to take her chances on the road even though she knows that means a different kind of threat. He insists she must come with them - that there is "real danger" on the road. There are bandits in the mountains of Mexico and any woman who is alone - especially a gringa - is fair game.

Flight takes many forms. Jane goes behind the little gas station to the bushes by a stream and sits down on a rock. She takes several deep breaths and turns completely in on herself. She looks around that wonderful scenery with the small rocks and hills and clear blue water and begins to breathe fully.

Until that moment, Jane has never meditated. She does not believe in God and she is absolutely awash in emotional responses to life. The God she has been raised with wouldn't have had anything to do with the woman she had become.

Yet, Jane is able to turn within and find peace immediately. She is able to quiet her mind and connect with some Source on which she can rely. She feels that Source in the rocks and water and sky. She feels that Source all around her and within her. It isn't as if she has found answers to her problems. It is that for a moment or two, she has truly transcended her situation and feels at one with the Infinite. She is in Peace.

She sits quietly, with her feet in the cold mountain water and lets Peace wash through her. After about twenty minutes of gifted illumination, she gets back into the car and rides down the mountains with them.

By the time they are back in Oaxaca, the wife is calmed down and apologizing for spoiling their trip. This is Jane's cue to pretend everything is all right, but she does not.

Almost twenty years have passed. Jane has forgiven herself, the man, and his wife (who is long ago dead). The screams have faded, but what hasn't faded is the flame of peace which Jane found within herself when she was in real trouble. Jane can still remember exactly what it felt like to sit on that rock with her feet in that cold mountain stream and rely on a Source greater than herself. It felt very sure, very true, and very honest. Jane now thinks of herself as an honest woman.

****

That day in the mountains of Mexico when I contacted a Source of Peace which I later learned to call God was the beginning of a whole new relationship with life for me. It was the beginning of my understanding that there really is a Source of Life which I can contact and rely upon. Dr. Ernest Holmes, founder of Religious

133

Science, puts it this way, "There is a Power for Good in the Universe and you can use it."

As a spiritual counselor, I now have the opportunity to work with many women who have problems. As they talk, I see that they are knee-deep in trouble and I understand that they are feeling overwhelmed. Because I have been there and done that, I also know they have more to rely upon than they think.

I would like to tell every woman in the whole world, "You have the power to feel connected to a wonderful Source of Love, of Power and of Joy. You are already in touch with God. God lives in your heart and mind and God is as near to you as your next breath. No matter how wounded you feel, no matter how damaged or shamed you feel, no matter what you have done or where you have been, you are the Beloved. You are wonderful! You are perfect! You are complete! And you are Love!"

I listen to women's stories and I try to recapture my sense of Peace and Love as I experienced it the day I transcended my troubles in the mountains of Oaxaca. I quietly hold a vision of peace and love for the person who is talking and mentally transcend their problems by contacting the Truth.

Through my spiritual studies I have learned that Peace always answers when you call, that Love always answers when you are open and that any condition, history or belief can be healed by the Power which lives in each of us. That power is our God-given birthright.

Over the years, I have come to understand the story of the Prodigal Daughter (my personal adaption of the Bible story) as my story. To come home is simply to turn to God, which is simply to turn within to feel the Infinite Source of Love. To feel the Peace that Passes Understanding is to know the truth about yourself. No matter what is going on in your life, you are at one with your Source. Whenever you open up to Love, it rushes to fill your need. And most of all - no matter how sticky a problem feels, it is simply surface stuff. You are the Beloved.

As a result of my spiritual understanding, I think of the word self-reliant as meaning a reliance on the Source of Power which is within me. I believe we are all really much greater than any role we choose to play in life.

We are in communication with a truth much greater and deeper than we may know. We may or may not know about God, but God is accessible at any moment. It is a Power for Good and we can use it to turn anything we want to turn around.

I have never again been as emotionally fragile as I was that afternoon in the Oaxacan mountains. I now realize that relationship triggered old, unsolved relationship issues from my childhood and I have spent some time and energy straightening my "stuff" out. I also realize that I was deeply upset because I wasn't living up to my own set of values. Whenever we are living a lie, living outside our own belief system, we are bound to create suffering for ourselves. I was also very fragile because I had just given up my reliance on alcohol.

Nevertheless, in that twenty-minute period, I had a wonderful understanding that I was much, much more than I had ever guessed. The little self who was in so much pain was nothing compared to the real me. The Real Self I was able to lean on was a deeper, stronger self than any surface reality. For that twenty minutes, I let that Real Self permeate my whole being and experience. I was shining with the truth.

Today, I have strong feelings of self-worth and self-love. I am a very self-reliant person and for me, self-reliance means I do not look to the outside for approval or advice. I simply turn to Divine Light which burns brighter and brighter within me. Each time I turn inward I feed the flame and allow it to burn brighter.

Within me is a Divine Spark which longs to love me and allow my total life to be filled with illumination - with what other teachers have called the Christ Presence. That Divine Spark is my true nature and it has always been with me, though there were certainly times in my life when I could not feel its flame. It was always there and I could call on it when I willed it. God's light never failed me when I called on it, no matter what I was up to.

****

QUESTIONS

1. Is there any behavior in your life which feels dishonest now?

2. What is your way of dealing with difficult situations?

3. Do you have any memories of contacting that quiet place within while in difficulty?

AFFIRMATIONS

I am the Beloved.

I am centered in a quiet Truth on which I can rely.

I rely on my Source for strength and wisdom.

I am perfect, whole and complete. God and I are One.

CHAPTER
EIGHTEEN

WISE WOMEN
WATCH THEIR LIGHTING

It is 1973. Jane is 40 years old. She is walking down the street in Oaxaca. The sun is shining, but it is two-thirty in the afternoon and she is on the shady side of the street. It is cold and the wind is blowing.

Jane shivers and wishes she had a sweater. It was warm when she started out this morning but now it is almost cold. She shivers and wishes she were someplace else. She would go back downtown and take a taxi home but she knows the walk is good for her. One reason why she is not trying to buy a car down here is that she likes the exercise she gets from walking.

She walks faster and that helps a little bit, but not much. She tries to concentrate on the wonderful flowers that she sees along the way. It is October and *everywhere there are deep red feathery blooms which she has been told are called Coxcomb. The Mexicans call them the Blood of Christ. <u>Sangre de Christo</u> sounds a bit better, but she wishes the flowers had a happier name.*

She is walking home in exactly the same way she always does, taking the route which leads her by the Cathedral and then goes up the hill to the newer <u>colonias</u>. Along the way she will pass giant Tule trees. Their trunks are so large that they seem to crawl like living things along the sidewalks. Jane thinks again of the blood red flowers. Then she thinks of the twisted trunks of the Tule trees. This is a strange land and she is cold and alone. She wishes she had never come here.

She shivers and wraps her arms around herself, hugging her chest as though she were a small girl. The country is so Catholic. Everywhere she looks there is another church, another cathedral and everywhere she looks she sees that she is a stranger. It's all very depressing.

<u>Gringa</u> - the word is irritating and means nothing. It is as if no one can see her because she is from a foreign country. Better when they call her <u>Professora</u>, that at least has some dignity to it. What she would like more than anything is for someone to call her by her real name. This cold day, she wishes with all her heart that she were in a more familiar place, doing familiar things. The streets feel crowded and dirty. The walls of the houses are covered with multi-colored plaster and they

appear to be a historic hodgepodge. Jane wonders why they don't at least cover the old coat of plaster with one of the same color if they're not going to do a good job of covering up. Her house in Redondo Beach is a regular tract house with pale green shutters and a narrow strip of lawn. She wonders if the tenants are keeping up the lawn.

Though she seldom thinks of home, she wonders what her friends are doing today. What about her family? She frowns as she thinks about her family. The news is not good, but then the news has never been good. She thinks about the book she is trying to write. It is not going well. She has made a mistake to think she can write about something as complicated as her college years. It is all a mistake.

The wind is really sharp now and she thinks of going into a coffee shop for a cup of coffee. Or she might have a beer and then walk home. A cold beer won't warm her up, but it might cheer her up. She isn't sure....

Suddenly, it occurs to her that she could cross to the other side of the street. There is no rule that says she has to continue walking on the left side just because she always has. She laughs out loud and crosses the street.

Now she is in the direct sunshine and that makes all the difference. She feels the warm sun on her back and she knows she will soon be quite warm. Over here on this side of the street, the sky looks blue and the colors on the houses are bright yellows, greens, blues and pinks.

She loves the colors of Mexican plaster walls and she loves being here. She loves being a gringa.

****

Taking control of our thoughts is essentially just like crossing to the sunny side of the street. First, we must become conscious that we are stuck in an unpleasant train of thought, and then we must decide to cross over to a new track. We do it all the time and with practice, we can do it with habitual ease.

There is nothing that says you have to let your thoughts control you. You are <u>more than</u> your thought patterns and that <u>more than</u> has a stronger and firmer grip on your thoughts than you might believe.

If you are inclined to gloomy thoughts, you can train yourself to think about pleasant things. One simple way to get in the habit of doing this is to make a list of things you are grateful for. From time to time, perhaps once or twice a day if you feel you need the extra concentration, read the list aloud. Counting your blessings is a way of crossing to the sunny side of the street.

Try telling your life story and putting a positive spin on it. Writing your life story can be a fascinating project because the facts seem to shine and dance in the prevailing lighting. One day you can tell the story of how you and your dog ran away from home and make it be a comedy. On another day you can write it as a tragedy. Same dog - same story, but different lighting.

142

We are all the electrical engineers of our own lives. We shine the lights on our own reality. We can stay stuck in our role of victim and recount tale after tale of our miserable childhoods or we can turn on the lights and begin to enjoy some of the wonderful adventures we had as a kid.

We all have a certain quality of light in our lives and Wise Women make sure their light switches are in good working order. Ask yourself why you like to be around certain people. Isn't it because those certain people make you feel successful or pretty or just glad to be alive? When you are with people you like, you are letting your light shine full voltage and they respond.

Falling in love can be seen as a matter of letting your light shine for each other in a very special way. We are never more lit up than when we are in love and we attract our loved ones by the shining light in our eyes, the delightful laugh in our voice and the glow of our skin. Ask any woman and she will tell you that the very best beauty treatment is to fall in love.

With practice, we can be in love with life all the time. We can be in love with the world. We can learn to let our light shine brightly, let our eyes glow, our skin be luminous and our laughter be delightful. We can know ourselves well enough to know we are love and in that knowing - we can let our light truly shine.

To let one's light shine means to take charge of one's life. To let one's light shine means to make choices about how we live, who we spend time with, and most of all - what we think.

That story about crossing the street when you are cold is a metaphor for how to manage your life. When you are in an uncomfortable mood, do you just wait for the gloom to lift or do you cross the street and start to cheer up? When you are in a difficult relationship do you just endure or do you take steps?

****

QUESTIONS

1. When is my light brightest?

2. Are there people in my life who I always feel bright around?

3. Are there people in my life who I always feel dark around?

4. How much control do I actually have over my moods?

5. What could I do to gain more control over my moods?

6. If I decided to really let my light shine, what would I do differently?

AFFIRMATIONS

I let my light shine wherever I am.

I love life and life loves me.

I am love.

I am light.

I am love and light.

I am happy all of the time.

I am always on the sunny side of the street.

I make optimistic and intelligent choices.

I control my thoughts and direct my attention to positive matters.

CHAPTER
NINETEEN

WISE WOMEN
ARE PROSPEROUS

It is 1939. Jane is six years old. She is in Oklahoma City, visiting her mother's rich cousin, Zee Halliburton. Zee and her husband own Halliburton's Department store and they live in a hotel. Jane is very impressed.

Zee takes Jane to dinner in the hotel restaurant. She asks, "Can you read?" Jane nods her head. Zee is pleased and she says, "Well, read the menu. You can have anything you want."

The words wash over Jane with a amazing impact. It is an absolutely new concept. She has never known anyone who wasn't worried to death about money, has never known anyone who casually accepts the good linen, shining silver and polite waiters as part of the daily routine. She has never been in a fancy hotel before, nor has she been in an expensive restaurant.

The sensory impressions might be overwhelming except Jane is so happy here. She feels she is in her right place. She snuggles into her chair and takes her time ordering, choosing chicken and apple pie with cheese.

It is a very satisfactory meal and her whole four-day visit is just splendid. She is given some new clothes and taken around to be shown off. She enjoys the whole experience but most of all, she will remember the sensation of being told, "You can have anything you want."

****

One of the great joys of writing in a journal or writing about your own life is that you figure out where your most effective and best ideas come from. I had forgotten all about that trip to Oklahoma City until one night, in a prosperity class at a Religious Science church, I was asked to write about my vision of true wealth. My vision included living in a hotel and as I talked about that, I remembered the Halliburtons, who gave me the only introduction to the concept of wealth that I would have for many, many years.

The phrase, "You can have anything you want," is the wealthiest statement one can make.

Reverend Carol Carnes of Calgary, Canada tells the story of her youngest brother being taken to a fish restaurant before he could read. His parents told him, "You can have any kind of fish you want."

The little boy thought about it for a while and said, "I'll take a whale."

In my prosperity classes, I have used a guided meditation in which I asked people to imagine that they were in the Universe Cafe and they could order anything they wanted. Then I went on to explain that what we can desire, envision, and mentally accept, we can achieve. Recently, I borrowed an enlarged version of that from a writer who said life was more like a cafeteria and we had to wait on ourselves.

While we probably can't quite manage whales and we may have to wait on ourselves, the concept of being able to choose is an important one. Try thinking of your life as a giant salad bar and seeing yourself picking out the lettuce and tomatoes and leaving the pickled corn and peppers behind. You don't have to take just any old thing to keep from starving to death. There is plenty to go around. You can pick and choose and have the best.

I think women face some special challenges when they begin to express more prosperity in their lives. Not only do they have to eliminate limiting ideas such as those which center around lack and limitation, but they have a whole set of extra beliefs around finding validation in love.

Are you willing to make more money than your husband? Are you willing to earn enough to support yourself in the style to which you wish to become accustomed? Does your ideal relationship include having the other person support you? Part of becoming prosperous is becoming self-reliant.

Dependency patterns show up in relationships, in financial matters, in health and even in our spiritual lives. We must insist on validating ourselves, we must insist on being self-reliant and we must insist on being financially independent.

What does financial independence look like? For one thing, it is based on a sure and certain knowledge that the basis of all wealth is the One Source. Every Wise Woman can say, "God is the Source of all my wealth." Your paycheck may come from McDonald's, but behind that paycheck is the flow of Divine Intelligence. Your husband may pay the bills and sign the checks, but behind his ability to do that is your connection to Infinite Wisdom.

Whether you are part of a couple in which there is only one bread winner, whether you have inherited wealth, whether you barely make the mortgage each month or you have millions of dollars in your estate, the ultimate source of your financial wealth is the ultimate source of your life. God is the creator of all wealth and God is never limited.

There are excellent prosperity books on finances available in any metaphysical bookstore. They all contain the same prosperity principles but they are written in a variety of styles. One of the most valuable is *Prosperous*

Woman by Dr. Ruth Ross. See the bibliography for a few other suggestions.

I believe guided meditations are a very effective and fast way to enlarge your capacity to accept the best in financial freedom. Write for a Cornucopia catalog of my guided meditations.

Here is a summary of some excellent financial information based on basic metaphysical principles.

1. There is enough to go around. We live in an abundant universe.

2. Prosperity is another word for freedom and making intelligent choices.

3. Money is created by intelligence and Creative Intelligence is unlimited.

4. You can have what you can accept emotionally and mentally.

5. Circulation is the key to continuous prosperity. Express gratitude through tithing or some other circulating action.

6. Ideas create money. You have access to excellent ideas by looking within.

7. Let go of old ideas which may be standing in the way of your financial prosperity.

8. You are attracting the level of prosperity which you currently believe you deserve or can attain. For more prosperity, you must raise your self-limiting belief systems.

****

QUESTIONS

1. Which of these prosperity principles is easy for you to believe? Why?

2. Are any of these prosperity principles difficult for you to accept? Why?

3. What ideas do you believe you could change in order to raise your prosperity level?

AFFIRMATIONS

I am a rich woman.

I am a wealthy woman who is surrounded by love, beauty and fun.

I live an opulent existence and I love it!

I am self-reliant in all matters, including money.

Money loves me and I love money.

CHAPTER
TWENTY

WISE WOMEN
ARE PERSISTENT

It is 1977. Jane is 44 years old. She is living in Pittsfield, Massachusetts, trying to build a writing career. She is also looking for a job and not having much success on either count. But Jane has recently rediscovered metaphysics and she is using affirmations to change her life.

Her apartment is small and cluttered, filled with second hand furniture, paperback books and signs and cards pasted on the walls. The cards say things such as; Jane is a winner! Jane is a talented writer who is well paid for her work. Jane is selling everything she writes now. Jane has several good clients who buy all her work. Jane is a success. Jane is an excellent writer and her work is well recognized.

Jane has ten years of unsuccessful writing behind her and she is trying very, very hard not to be discouraged. She is working on her writing fifteen to twenty-five hours a week, keeping records of what she writes and she has recently had just a little success. She has sold five short stories and two very small easy reader novels to Scholastic Books. She has also sold some very short feature articles to the local newspaper.

Now she is working on some more short stories, waiting to hear about the two sample chapters and outline she sent to a new editor at Scholastic. If this woman takes her idea, it will mean moving up into trade paperbacks and it will mean more money and more sales. Jane wants her idea to be accepted so badly that she is afraid to think about it.

The mail comes at noon and there is a rejection letter from the new editor. She says she didn't like the story because the characters are too stereotypical, the plot is too thin and the writing is too choppy. She doesn't say to try her again.

Jane cries for several hours. She is so tired of all the rejection she has accumulated over the years and she really wanted to make this next step into a different level of writing. She wishes with all her heart that things had been different.

Eventually, she stops crying and begins to read all the signs on her walls. She then picks up her favorite metaphysical book, _The Power of Decision_ by Dr. Raymond Charles Barker, and reads it until she falls *asleep. The next morning she writes the editor a letter thanking her for the excellent suggestions (there really weren't any) and saying she'll have the rewrite on her desk within the month (the editor didn't ask for a rewrite).*

Three weeks later Jane sends a rewritten manuscript. This one is carefully patterned on the work of other authors who are doing what Jane wants to be doing. The outline is immediately accepted and Jane writes the book. Within fifteen years she will have done seventeen books for this editor.

****

Life always gives you an opportunity to reconfirm your commitment to your goals. Whether you choose something as difficult as being a writer or simply want to finish a night-school class in computer skills, sooner or later, you will have to make a crucial decision to continue on your course.

Ask any happily married couples who are celebrating their twentieth or fiftieth anniversary how they've done so well. If they are honest, they will tell you that they had plenty of chances to bail out of the bargain. Most will say they even thought about it once or twice.

Life goes in the direction you give it, but it doesn't always go straight ahead. Only in retrospect can we see that our journey was inevitable. In the short term, there are plenty of places to turn back or change our minds.

Once we set goals it is very, very important that we make it a definite plan to stick with those goals for a certain amount of time. In my case, I was not prepared to let go of the dream of writing even though I'd been at it for ten years. I made that decision to stick with the dream because I encountered some new information about how to establish a business-like approach to my desired activity. I also made that decision because my metaphysical reading convinced me that where there was intense desire, there would be a way.

Before you undertake a difficult task such as building a successful marriage, completing college, establishing your own business or getting into the theater, ask yourself if you have a definite desire to complete the activity. Few of us get very far on a whim.

The deeper the desire, the clearer it is to me that a woman will find the way and the talent to achieve whatever it is she hopes to achieve. One simple thing you can do for yourself is to state your goals in clear cut language and constantly reinforce those goals with affirmations, reminders and reinforcement for your thought patterns. When you meet with disappointment, don't let it sink you. Feel the disappointment and go on.

I once heard a motivational real estate salesperson talking about how to handle rejection. He said, "If you knock on forty doors and get turned down, tell yourself that you are forty doors closer to yes."

Rejection is natural when you are trying to do something new. Don't take it personally and use any tips you can get from the rejection experiences to move ahead. While I was a sales manager, I had sales agents who didn't get the job call me and ask what they could learn from the interview experience. I gladly told them why I hired someone else and I assume they used the information to find excellent jobs elsewhere.

Many women are entirely too passive when they are job hunting. You are there because you want a job, so why not try and convince the prospective employer you are the answer to her problems? As a sales and marketing director, I was always looking for really good sales agents. It amazed me how few of them tried to "sell" me on themselves. If they couldn't sell themselves, how could they sell my product?

When you go on a job interview, do you make it your business to know something about the company before you actually talk to anyone? A few well-placed, intelligent questions can really help you get the job. Do your homework and be alert.

Achieving your goals is part of a general pattern of taking charge of your life. You can do it. You can successfully reprogram your thoughts so that your general expectation is one of success. You can stay alert and learn enough to be a solution to someone's problem. You can give good enough service to invite return business. All it requires is a pro-active and persistent attitude toward life and work. Go for it!

****

QUESTIONS

1. Do you consider yourself a persistent person?

2. If you were more persistent, what would you be doing right now?

3. What goals have you achieved because of your commitment, intense desire or persistence?

4. Do you use affirmations and reminders to help you stay on track in your work?

5. If you were to design a special message to hang on your wall, what would it say?

AFFIRMATIONS

I am pro-active.

Rejection isn't in my vocabulary.

I handle setbacks with ease.

I go all out for what I want and I get it.

I am a persistent person.

CHAPTER
TWENTY-ONE

WISE WOMEN ARE DIRECT

It is 1982. Jane is 49 years old. She is interviewing a woman for a book she is writing on successful second marriages. This particular woman is talking about how she went about finding the right man after her husband left her.

Jane notices that the woman is pleasant looking but not beautiful. She has been a church secretary and now she is a housewife. She has married a wealthy shopkeeper - a man who was born here in this small southern town as she was. She says, "I went out with a few engineers who were from the east, but I decided I really just like good old boys. So I stopped dating engineers and went for the locals - friends of friends."

Jane notes that the woman seems perfectly comfortable describing her efforts to meet men. Jane says, "You seem to have figured it all out."

"I did," the woman replies. "I joined Parents Without Partners and the church singles group and I called all my friends. I made it my goal to meet a new single man every week. I figured one of them would do."

"So what about the man you married, was it love at first sight?"

"Not really. I had been dating a man I met at Parents Without Partners and there were some things I liked better about him. But we dated for three months and it was clear he didn't want to get married. I told him I wouldn't see him any more and then George came into my life. I guess I was too broken up about the other one to see how great George was at first."

"How long did it take you?"

"About three dates. By that time, I knew he wanted to get married and so did I. We were about the same age and we came from the same background. We had a lot in common and we could laugh a lot."

"So you married George?"

"Of course."

****

Several years ago I was working on a book project which required me to talk with two hundred women who had made successful second marriages. I toured the country, listening to stories in small towns, suburbs and cities and I listened to story after story which involved change, growth and courage.

I talked with a few widows but most of the women were divorced. They lived in California, Maryland, Massachusetts, New York, Texas, Virginia and Wisconsin. They ranged in age from late twenties to late eighties and their educational level went from 10th grade dropout to graduate school.

Some were housewives who had been on welfare or in low-paying jobs before they married the second time. Others had successful careers and marriage was not an economic necessity, but it was the frosting on their Life's Cake.

They were very different from each other and each of them defined herself as happy in her second marriage. As they talked about their lives, I discovered that nearly all were remarkable women. Listening to their stories taught me how emotionally strong women are.

I learned that, almost without exception, women who wanted to remarry were quite direct about it. They went after what they wanted with no shame, no equivocation and no self-doubt. They didn't expect themselves or the men they would marry to be perfect - just better than the last one.

Those women believed in marriage and they didn't waste their time with married men, with lounge lizards or any other variety of unacceptable companions. They wanted to be married and they weren't ashamed to say that was their goal.

All of the women went through emotional and spiritual changes before they got to the place where they were ready to make a good marriage. While some presented their stories as simple, "And then I found the right guy and lived happily ever after," the patterns were clearly visible under the platitudes.

I remember a legal secretary in Washington, D.C., who had been a debutante. She had married a rich boy and been dumped by him two years later. She was selling Mary Kay cosmetics when I met her and her values seemed to me to be an only slightly updated version of Scarlet O'Hara's.

Nevertheless, she had to change and grow before she made her happy marriage. As she told me her story, her true feelings about being treated as an object by the rich and powerful men she was dating in Washington began to come out. At one point, she referred to herself as an "armpiece." Somehow, she struggled through the humiliation of thinking her self-worth depended only on how she looked and found some spiritual basis for her life. Tired of being used and abused, she joined a church and eventually married a mechanic who was good to her. "He really likes me," she confided.

Most of the women I talked to had deeper and stronger values than debutante balls and the latest cosmetics, but they all wanted to be "really liked." Their stories usually contained an element of learning to really like themselves before this could happen.

I talked to a Russian Countess who fled the 1918 revolution and came to America with her infant son. She suffered, Russian style, and had a long career in the arts.

When she was in her 50s she remarried and moved to the suburbs to live happily ever after.

I talked to a country girl who went home from her favorite bar with a different man each night. Despite the odds, she finally found the right guy. She was willing to break out of the pickup truck culture she'd been born into and go home with a hippie whose values allowed him to respect her. She still thought he was a "freak," but she loved him and he loved her.

I talked to school teachers, corporate executives, and a labor union organizer. Everyone had a fascinating and unique story. Some, like the country girl, I understood quite well. Others were a mystery to me.

I was amazed at how easy marriage seemed to be for these women who had made successful marriages. At that time in my life I was one of many women in my educational and age group who were involved in long, difficult relationships. My friends and I were thinking about "fixing" our relationships and spoke openly of "working on the relationship" as though it were a second job to be handled in the evenings.

After I talked to those 200 women, I decided that most of my group of friends were more interested in the drama than the happy endings. We didn't really want to be married, we just wanted to be romantically involved. I stopped saying I wanted to get married. It was obviously a lie. I'd been married only four years in my life, so it couldn't have been a high priority for me. I even stopped complaining about the relationship I was in.

So, in one half year of my life, perhaps because I was studying metaphysics and ready to learn, I learned a few simple things about going after the relationship you really want. I learned that people who want to be happily married put the priority of marriage <u>before</u> romantic love. I learned that women who approached the subject of marriage logically were quite happy with the results. I also learned that I could stop kidding myself and the sky wouldn't fall in.

One piece of fallout information came when I discovered that self-help, spiritual and inspirational books really do change lives. Time after time, as I was listening to some woman's story, I heard about her dark night of the soul and then I heard her say, "So then a friend gave me this book about how to be your own best friend and I did that."

"You did what?" I would ask.

"I decided to be my own best friend and I did what the book said to do." the answer would come back.

It wasn't just one book title that worked. It seemed as though they could draw inspiration from any number of metaphysical, religious or just ordinary self-help books. They quoted the *Bible, The Art of Loving, How To Be Your Own Best Friend*, and *Your Erroneous Zones*. Everyone seemed to be able to find wisdom in a book if she was ready to change.

Many of them found groups to support their search and to support their change. Several women found friends and even husbands in church singles groups.

164

Several sought out non-denominational groups such as Parents Without Partners.

While these women were generally less well-educated or sophisticated than my personal friends, I quickly saw that they were true heroines. I became convinced that many women live heroic lives as they quietly care for their children, their elderly parents, and their spouses. As I toured the country, listening to stories, I was deeply impressed by the clarity, assertiveness and courage of these _ordinary_ women.

I remember one woman who was married to a minister in a traditional church for twenty years. He was a philanderer and she kept his secret despite the fact that he lost two pulpits. Finally, when he was in his mid-forties, he ran away with a Sunday School teacher and left her and her three boys with no support. She never heard from him again.

This woman went to work for minimum wage in a pharmacy and continued to attend the same church. She joined a chorus and met a man she eventually married. Only after they were married did she discover that he had a million dollars. As she told her story, she seemed to accept it as a fairly normal life and she was certainly a normal looking woman. But the story remained one of the wildest ones I heard!

The experience of listening to those women's stories convinced me that any woman who wishes to make a good marriage can do it as soon as she has established enough self-love and self-respect to know what she wants and go after it.

If I hadn't already known the value of setting goals and taking action, the investigation would have convinced me.

****

QUESTIONS

1. What is my current belief about my relationship?

2. What would I like to change in my current situation?

3. What am I doing to further my goals?

4. What could I do to further my goals?

5. What beliefs about myself would I like to change?

AFFIRMATIONS

I am a loving person who attracts love into my life.

I am now attracting the perfect right partner into my life.

Successful marriage is my goal and Divine Intelligence knows how to bring the correct opportunities into my life.

CHAPTER
TWENTY-TWO

WISE WOMEN
DON'T BEAR GUILT

It is 1986. Jane is 53 years old. She has picked up her friends at the airport and she is driving them around San Diego, showing them the sights. The sky is gloomy and the day is dark. They drive to the top of Point Loma, but it begins to rain and it is obviously pointless to get out and look at the harbor.

Jane says, "I'm so sorry about this weather." Suddenly, something clicks in her brain and she begins to laugh. She realizes she has been apologizing about the weather all afternoon. She has been reading Emerson's essays in her Science of Mind class and she remembers his phrase, My life is not an apology. At the time, Jane had thought, But a lot of mine is. Since then, she has programmed herself to notice any patterns of guilt.

This one is so funny it makes her laugh. She says to her friends, "Of course, I didn't order this weather for you. My birthday may be Earth Day but I haven't quite turned into Mother Nature." They go home to a warm fire, leaving sightseeing for another day.

Jane decides she will never apologize for the weather again. It isn't her fault.

****

Learning to take responsibility for one's actions is a major part of developing wisdom. Learning to ignore old patterns of accepting guilt for things you didn't cause is another wonderful step along the path.

Many of us ingest guilt in toxic doses as children. The subliminal message behind being told we should feel guilty when our muddy feet get the kitchen floor dirty, is that we should feel guilty whenever mother is unhappy. Some of us get an even deeper, more damaging message that we should feel guilty for being here at all.

We are told that guilt is sometimes necessary. Theoretically, people who have no capacity to feel guilt have no limits to the ways in which they harm each other. That may be so in a few clinical cases, but the people I meet in my world need to lighten up their guilt load. They all have plenty of built-in controls and guilt slows them down in their quest for a wonderful life. Guilt not only slows us down, it can confuse and paralyze.

170

Do you apologize for the weather? If you give a party and someone doesn't have a good time, do you feel guilty? If your mother calls twice a day and you want to ask her to call only twice a week, does guilt keep you from doing it?

If your son fails math do you feel guilty? If your daughter inherits your wide hips do you feel guilty? If you don't have enough money to send your nephew to Harvard do you feel guilty? If people are starving in Somalia do you feel guilty?

Questions such as these are a good way to approach the <u>habit</u> of guilt and begin to separate reality from fantasy and distinguish the true limits of our responsibility. It is childish grandiosity to assume responsibility for things we cannot possibly control, such as someone else's temper. Nowhere does the serenity prayer, <u>God grant me serenity to accept the things I cannot change, courage to change the things I can and wisdom to know the difference</u>, seem more appropriate.

It takes courage to bring the cake that didn't rise to the party without guilt. It takes serenity to accept that you'll never sing as well as Whitney Houston. It takes wisdom to live a good guilt-free life.

One happy outcome of all the work women and men have done on family structure and inventing new roles for ourselves is a general amnesty from guilt for own fathers and mothers. As we struggle to live more whole and more solid lives than they were able to, we see what challenges they faced in the Beaver Cleaver days.

One of my wisest mentors once told me I was responsible for my actions but not the outcome. The point he was making was that I just needed to be sure that my actions were taken in love, from a place of authenticity, and that the outcome would be up to the Higher Power.

Over the years, I have come to understand that my thoughts are a part of my actions and that habitual patterns of guilt have created unpleasant situations in my life. Life (or God) responds to mental messages which it receives and if those messages are a constant bombardment of I'm not worthy, I didn't try hard enough, I could have done better, then Life will continue to present opportunities for feeling guilty.

Women sometimes co-opt this basic metaphysical principle and use it to feel even more guilty about themselves. They read or hear that they can create their own lives and then they catch a cold. Instead of focussing on creating health, they use the cold as an excuse to feel worse. Guilt is invasive, insidious and useless. Wouldn't you rather be healthy?

If one does catch a cold, it is better to avoid feeling guilty about it. We can, however, accept responsibility for establishing a mental model of health. Don't moan and groan about the illness, don't talk about the symptoms or diagnose the reasons for the cold. Just take good care of yourself and love yourself. You can't feel guilty about being sick and establish a model of health in your mind at the same time.

Eliminating habitually negative thought patterns is wise. Feeling guilt when something comes up that you don't like is nonsense. If you don't like it, change it. You can do that.

****

QUESTIONS

1. Can you imagine yourself apologizing if it rains?

2. Can you imagine taking credit for the sun shining?

3. Do you see any place where guilt is keeping you stuck?

4. If you could eliminate the guilt, what would you change in your life?

AFFIRMATIONS

I release all guilt about the past. I am wonderful right NOW.

Guilt neither controls nor motivates me. I act out of love.

I release guilt and convert the energy to more wisdom power.

CHAPTER
TWENTY-THREE

WISE WOMEN BELIEVE LIFE
IS SUPER AND NATURAL

The year is 1994. Jane is 61 years old. She is staying all night in a hotel in Los Angeles, attending a weekend jazz concert. She rises early and goes down to the lobby to see if she can find a cup of coffee. It is 6:30 a.m.

She finds coffee in the lobby and a few travelers who are sitting around, waiting for the airport shuttle. They are reading newspapers and listening to piano music. The music is great jazz and Jane wonders how they talked any of the musicians into staying up so late or getting up so early. She walks closer to the piano and laughs aloud.

The piano is playing all by itself! When she was a kid, Jane went to horror movies in which a piano playing by itself meant a ghost was in the haunted house. These days, it only means the hotel is up-to-date on computer capabilities.

****

Do you believe in ghosts? In fate or destiny? Do you spend money on fortune tellers? Do you own a ouija board? How about Tarot cards? Do you read your horoscope in the newspaper? Most of us would answer yes to one or more of those questions, but I certainly hope we don't make our major decisions based on what the ouija board tells us. Do we?

Traditionally, feminine wisdom is associated with spiritual and/or occult powers and many women choose the non-traditional spiritual route as a path to wisdom. Experimenting with psychic powers can open you up to the wonderful, unlimited ability of your own mind. It can also show you how marvelously connected you are to life and to others. Mostly, however, it is a blind alley where you can waste a lot of time that you could be spending on getting ahead with your life.

Talk to angels if you need a hobby. Pay your bills on time and don't rely on the angels to sweeten the disposition of the credit manager. You won't need miracles or supernatural help if you really catch hold of the wonderful truth that there is a Power For Good in the Universe and you are using it in your life. You have the power to influence your fate without intermediaries.

176

I personally would never suggest anyone try channeling, mostly because I think it as foolish to give up your power to outside spirit entities as it is to turn it over to your next-door neighbor. I would also suggest you never blindly believe or obey any guru, spiritual teacher, channeler, or psychic. For that matter - don't do what your next door neighbor or your best friend tells unless you really think it through for yourself. Playing gullible can be dangerous and it is really just another variation of playing victim.

I'm absolutely certain the path to wisdom is through accepting and developing one's own ability to exercise personal power and that self-reliance is the only permanent answer to developing maturity.

It is sad and foolish to spend time and energy on magic potions or fortune tellers to keep from dealing with your life. I once knew a woman who had some chronic issues about dependency, solitude and depression. She wasn't living the life she wanted and she could never quite work up the nerve to change things. She was afraid to risk so she coped.

Whenever she was really restless and unhappy, she would go to a fortune teller and have her future told. She always went to very expensive ones and the fortune tellers always told her what any shy, single, middle-aged woman wanted to hear. She would come home believing she was soon going to meet the man of her dreams. That would keep her going another six months or year. Tragically, this pattern went on for twenty years.

A lot of women are interested in exploring Goddess Power. That seems to me to be an interesting approach to a spiritual life. Again, it is as good as the group and the leader you find. A group built on the hatred of men and a belief in the victimization of women is only a slight improvement over going to an "old-time religion" where God talks to the minister, the minister talks to the husband and the husband talks to his wife. It is far from whole or healthy.

I would say this about exploring the so-called supernatural - if it opens you up to your own natural powers, that's fine. If it creates or keeps dependency patterns going, that's something you really will need to reconsider before you get very far in your work on becoming a Wise Woman.

Experimentation is fun. So - yes to learning to use the pictures on the Tarot deck to open up your own abilities, no to running to your local reader to find out whether you should marry Tom, Dick or Harry.

Women who wish for good luck, carry rabbit's feet, go to fortune tellers or dream of the man who is their fate are all involved in some kind of belief in a power or powers outside themself having the ability to shape their destiny.

Sooner or later (and I hope it is sooner) you will be moving away from any beliefs in outside forces manipulating your life. Once you accept that the power which is moving your life is within you, you can accept a super life.

The belief that there are seers who can peer into the future and see what is going to happen to someone is usually based on a belief that life is all programmed before the event - that there is no real choice and no free will. All you have to do is look outside yourself at the events in other people's lives to see that the choices people make today are shaping their lives tomorrow. If your friends' choices are so clearly shaping their lives, how can you deny that your choices are shaping yours?

Some of us would rather believe in luck, in ghosts, in hexes, in magic charms, in horoscopes and in fortune tellers than face the task of changing our own lives. Here's the good news - you don't have to change your life. It will change automatically when you change your thinking.

There are laws of cause and effect operating in our lives. Those laws are clear, they are powerful and they can be employed in every area of life. How we think about ourselves will be mirrored in how people treat us. How we think about others will be mirrored in the kind of people we attract. If we believe we are lucky, things will go better than if we believe we are lightning rods for bad luck.

Focus on your thinking. Make sure you program yourself to believe you are lucky. If you win a trip to Bermuda, don't say, "I can't believe I won it! Instead, say, "Isn't that super and natural!"

Refer to yourself as a winner in every area of your life. Notice your good luck and accept it as natural.

Never, never say you are unlucky. Say you are super and you are natural!

****

QUESTIONS

1. Have you ever gone to a fortune teller? How did it feel?

2. Do you relate to the expression, "I make my own luck."

AFFIRMATIONS

I make my own luck.

I am creating my future by my current thoughts and choices.

I was born under a lucky star.

This is my lucky day.

CHAPTER
TWENTY-FOUR

WISE WOMEN
SPEAK FOR THEMSELVES

It is 1964. Jane is 31 years old. She is entertaining a colleague of her husband's on their back porch. The two of them are trying to scrape up a conversation after they've agreed the weather is warm and the Delaware River is high. Her task is to keep him entertained until her husband finishes his work. The colleague is waiting for him to finish so he can take it with him to a meeting tomorrow. Jane and the man are stuck with each other for an indefinite amount of time.

He asks, "Do you work?"

"Not anymore. I just do a little volunteer work and some substitute teaching."

"What kind of volunteer work do you do?"

"Oh, I'm on a few committees. Historical society, League of Women Voters, some other do-good things."

There is a long silence and he asks, "Does this area have interesting history? Was it settled by the Dutch?"

"Oh," Jane laughs and flutters her hands helplessly, "I'm not an expert on Bucks County history. I just make the punch at the meetings. I may be wrong, but I think that it was settled by the English and some Germans came later. But what would I know? I'm a California transplant." (laughter)

"Do you miss California?"

"I've never been anywhere until I moved here so I miss it a little. But my husband's work is here. The thing is, the people are so different on the east coast."

"How are they different?"

"Well, I really don't know much about it," Jane says, "but they just seem more stuck in their ways. Of course, I'm no expert."

"I think I'll take a walk downtown," the young man yawns as he rises. "Tell Dick I'll be back in an hour."

Jane stares into space as her husband's colleague walks away. She knows her husband was counting on her to keep this guy entertained and she has failed at the task.

****

Somehow, life's finishing school taught me to preface all my conversation with disclaimers. I've been working on that for thirty years and I still hear remnants of that nasty habit from time to time. The disclaimers went something like this;

"You'll probably think I'm crazy but...

"I'm not an expert but..."

"I really don't know much about it but..."

"You may be right but..."

"This may be a silly idea but..."

The list goes on and on. I now realize that the disclaimers served to defuse most of the power behind whatever it was that I wanted to say. I know that my early conversational style was built out of several threads of motivation - some historical, some regional, and some personal.

Historically, women of my generation were trained by women who believed their daughters' security and happiness depended on their pleasing manners. Therefore, mothers taught their daughters (by example and by definite instruction) that it was pleasing to act as though men were the real experts in life.

In compensation for this crippling behavior, our culture (and especially the Southern culture) gave us a compensatory belief in the power of a smart woman to manipulate and control men. Successful women worked behind the scenes. Heroines such as Scarlett O'Hara taught us how to use sexual attraction to get what we wanted. And then there were all those smart mothers who were the power behind the throne, from *Life With Father* on Broadway to *One Man's Family* on radio to

The Adventures or Ozzie and Harriet, on early TV, the father was manipulated and deceived. He seldom had a clue what was going on in the home that he kept supplied with bacon. Cartoons such as *Blondie and Dagwood* portrayed men as buffoons who didn't deserve direct communication.

I have come to believe that women whose roots were in the north and west learned more direct styles of communication than I did. My family was from Missouri and they thought of themselves as southerners. It seems to me that southern women of that day had a special regional tic of making little jokes about themselves which were followed by self-deprecating laughter. "What would I know? I'm a California transplant," is an example of a certain conversational style I still hear from perfectly intelligent women.

On a more personal level, I had a lot of childhood indoctrination which told me I was unacceptable. Like all children, I wanted to survive and to be loved. Since there was a great deal of competition between the women in my family, putting myself forward was problematic at best. My conversational patterns both reflected and reinforced an apparently submissive but manipulative personality and a low self-image. I am now an effective and powerful speaker. There are even times when I slip into that victim mentality - usually when I have failed to be as direct as I know I want to be. I still find many women complain they aren't heard.

In the 1990s many women continue to couch their opinions in conciliatory disclaimers. The power of our word is in directness, in conviction and in definite statements. We have no need for disclaimers.

I chose that scene with the strange young man from Atlanta because it put me at my worst. I was not allowed to talk about the work he and my husband were doing and indeed, I knew almost nothing about it. I was not allowed to flirt with a colleague of my husband's and I am certain he wouldn't have been interested anyway. He wasn't much of a conversationalist himself and so that afternoon was limited to what I could come up with.

Actually, I was fascinated by the east coast and I could have told him some delicious gossip about the people I'd met in Bucks County. I was also doing some fascinating volunteer work - I'd been to the State League of Women Voters as a delegate and was working with a group helping people who were being displaced by urban renewal programs in Trenton, New Jersey. My life was full of interesting opinions, activities and ideas, but I didn't have internal permission to tell him.

The sad part of the story is that I couldn't find the courage to share who I really was and what I was really doing with this stranger because I was afraid he wouldn't like me if I did. So I said almost nothing and consequently, he didn't like me!

We must learn to risk telling the truth about our strengths if we are ever to get what we want from life.

How can we hope to achieve equality, success and recognition if we continue to play conversational games from *Life With Father, Cinderella* or *Gone with the Wind?*

Let us live honestly and accept responsibility for the power of our words. People do believe what we tell them about ourselves. When we bracket our opinions with statements such as, "I don't know much about this..." it doesn't matter if we have a Ph.D. in the subject, they will nearly always believe the first part of the message.

As a student of metaphysics, I have learned the special power of the words, I AM. I believe they are a short prayer and that every time they are used, the Universe will respond at some level and Life will find a way to fulfill the statement.

Believing this, you can imagine that I am very careful what I say about myself these days, but there was a time when practically everything I said about myself was negative. Imagine the consequences of saying and thinking "I am no good" over a lifetime!

I can trace nearly every success I've had in my spiritual journey to my substitution of positive for negative after the words I AM.

I no longer say, "I am poor." I say, "I am rich." I no longer say, "I am old." I say "I am young at heart." I no longer say, "I am lost and confused," I say, "I am wise." I no longer say, "I am miserable," I say, "I am very happy." I no longer say, "I am fat," I say, "I am light."

Saying positive things about myself didn't come easily. Like many of you, I was taught that nice girls didn't push themselves forward, didn't brag and didn't attract attention by showing off. These attitudes are deeply ingrained in the psyches of many women and they show up in our conversation as well as our actions.

The place to institute change is at the level of core beliefs. We reflect our core beliefs every time we describe ourselves to the outside world.

So much has been written in the business world about women's need to be assertive, yet most young women still have trouble demanding credit for their ideas. I know many competent, even brilliant women who operate behind the scenes automatically. They get their projects approved and completed, but often their name is left off the credits. While they try to tell themselves that they got what they wanted, I can't help believing they really would have enjoyed recognition as well.

We can't always make people recognize our great work, but we can at least stop sabotaging ourselves. In my metaphysical classes, my students are usually required to give special reports on individual books or subjects which they share with the class. Their first task is to begin their presentation without apologizing. Unless reminded, many of them will begin their excellent work by telling how they didn't have time, they didn't get the right information, or that the book they needed was out of the library. Generally, women have a harder time giving a straightforward presentation.

One of my wonderful relatives makes delicious Thanksgiving dinners for the extended family. Each year, she does all the work, preparing a feast for people who love her and love her cooking. Each year, she insists that the turkey is too dry or the stuffing doesn't have enough oysters or the pies were lopsided. She is not fishing for compliments, she is asking for reassurance and in the process, she is stealing power from her beautiful gift. Just once, I would love to hear her say, "This is a perfect Thanksgiving dinner." The truth is, they always are.

Recently, there have been several studies and books about the differences between the conversational techniques of men and women. We are told that in many ways we speak a different language. We are told that women listen more. We are told that men interrupt more and tend to override what women are saying. Several of these studies and books have received a lot of attention.

It is good to be aware of ways in which women and men are different, but it is not enough to simply describe behavior. If the national consciousness is as interested as it seems to be in these language differences, it must mean that we are ready to change. Let us start the changes where we can - with ourselves.

Change must begin with you and me. It is not enough for women to sit around and be angry that men don't listen to them. We certainly can't sit around and whine that men should change. We must accept responsibility for what is coming out of our mouths.

Since I believe with all my heart and soul that my behavior will be mirrored back to me in my own life, I genuinely try to treat other people the way I want to be treated. The Golden Rule is golden because it is the basic rule of behavior in work, at home, and everywhere. The Golden Rule applies to dealing with men.

I would not want anyone to trick me, or to go behind my back, or to patronize me by letting me think I was getting my way while all the time the project was being stealthfully pushed forward. In short, I would choose honest, non-manipulative relationships with everyone in my life. Therefore, I am responsible for behaving in a straightforward, honest manner. As much as I can, I speak directly to any person in my life. I may not agree, but I try to honor them with direct communication.

Devious behavior is not life-affirming. It is better to speak up than to manipulate behind the scenes, no matter what your mother taught you. At least if you act honestly and ask directly for what you want, you will like yourself better.

Use your God-given imagination to practice speaking well of yourself. Spend a few quiet moments imagining yourself describing your work to your boss in such a way that you are certain he will hear you when you say you deserve a raise. Convince yourself and then act every day as though you know you deserve the best.

Try and imagine yourself in a situation where you are trying to say something and someone keeps interrupting

189

you. Imagine yourself telling that person to wait his (or her) turn. Imagine yourself simply raising your voice and overriding the other person's interruptions.

If you can't imagine yourself interrupting anyone, at least imagine a conversation where you actually say something nice about yourself.

Practice a little positive speaking in your real world. Even if it feels like bragging, make it a point to talk about something you do well from time to time. Pay attention to what you say about yourself and make sure it is positive. Don't say, "I know a little bit about computers," if you have been a computer nerd for years. Say, "I am an expert."

Though they are heard less, women are not really silent. Some are muted, of course, but most simply need to work on their delivery. They need to speak positively about themselves. They need to speak without disclaimers. They need to speak forcefully and with authority. They need to learn how to handle assertive behavior from others.

Some women need help in learning to listen. They have so much fear and old programming going on in their own heads that it operates like static and they can't actually pick up the messages that others are sending. Listening is a skill which comes easily to Wise Women because they are so quietly powerful they don't need to worry about static on the lines.

It is a fact that some women sabotage their effectiveness by talking too much about the wrong things.

They have been raised to play hostess in every situation and so they are apt to fill the airwaves before a business meeting with chatting about the kids or television programs. Even if you are chair of the committee, it is hard to gain the respect of your male colleagues if you've just been smoozing with the secretary about whether or not opaque pantyhose are warm enough for winter.

I know a lot of women feel very strongly that they don't want to imitate men's conversational styles. Nevertheless, they want the same jobs, the same pay and the same opportunities so they need to play at least some of the same game. There are times when silence makes a lot of sense.

Here is good advice for women who want to move ahead in an area where most of the bosses or leaders are men. Don't rattle on about nothing - they'll think you're an airhead. Stick to business. Say something positive about yourself when you can. And take your mother's advice and apply it to your own self. "If you can't say something nice, say nothing at all." These days, when the subject of mathematics comes up, I say nothing. I no longer feel it is necessary to confess that I haven't had math since the seventh grade or that I never could balance my checkbook. I talk about the things I can do, the things I do know.

Whether you are ambitious to move up the organizational ladder or not, remember that whatever you put behind <u>I Am</u> will be believed by most people. It also sends a powerful message to the Universe.

Your conversation is only one part of the way you speak for yourself, but it is a powerful creative force in your life. When your conversation about yourself is very positive, you will find your life is also much more positive. And remember that <u>I AM</u> is a magic ticket to wherever the words behind it put you. Make sure you want to go in that direction.

****

QUESTIONS

1. Can you imagine speaking up in opposition to anyone at a public meeting?

2. Have you ever spoken at a civic organization such as City Council, the PTA or Mothers Against Drunk Drivers? How did you feel about your effectiveness?

3. How do you think your conversational patterns might be impacting your work?

4. When someone interrupts you, what do you do? What do you think you might try next time?

5. Can you find any habit patterns in your speech which you wish to change? What are they?

6. Would you like to be heard more clearly? What might you do to change your pattern of speech?

AFFIRMATIONS

I speak freely and directly.

I am an excellent speaker.

I say only positive things about myself.

I have many good qualities and I am ready to tell the world about them.

I let my light shine freely.

CHAPTER
TWENTY-FIVE

WISE WOMEN
LOVE PLEASURE

It is 1967. Jane is 34 years old. She is in Tivoli Gardens in Copenhagen, Denmark for the fourth night in a row. She and her daughter and mother are on a ten-week tour of Europe and they have spent every Denmark evening in the same enchanting park. For all three of them, Tivoli Gardens is a wonderland of beauty and pleasure.

Jane wanders through the crowd, enchanted by the millions of sparkling lights, the wonderful flowers and the fabulous musicians. There are jugglers and street musicians and mimes everywhere. Tivoli Gardens is lit up with tiny magical lights that make it seem almost unreal. She thinks this is the most pleasant crowded place she has ever been. Everyone is cheerful and having fun. The atmosphere is pure delight.

Though they have tried to see as much of Europe as they could on their tour, the sounds and sights of Tivoli Gardens have drawn them back every evening. "Why go somewhere different when we know we love this?" she asks.

Last evening they saw the famous mime, Marcel Marceau, and later tonight they will see Marlene Dietrich. The great Marlene will perform as soon as it is dark. But at Tivoli Gardens, summer twilight seems to go on forever. Jane feels as though it really were an enchanted place and she is caught in the magical spell of dusk.

For Jane, the experience of drifting from flower bush to flower bush, cluster of people to small cafe, brightly lit dance pavilion to outdoor fountain is even more fascinating than seeing the shows. It is so different, so magical, that she sometimes has to remind herself she is really here.

She is deeply pleased she chose to take this trip. It was a big decision to spend her money to take the three of them on such an adventure. But she wanted to do it - to have a trip of a lifetime while her mother is young enough and her daughter is still with her. This is a major adventure for all three and it has been amazingly easy. No cross words and much delight.

Europe has been an enchanting melange of color, light and sound. So many wonderful paintings. So many wonderful towns. It is a dream come true and there is another month to come. When they leave Copenhagen tomorrow, they will go to England and then to Ireland.

Jane sighs and promises herself that she will remember what great fun life can be when you let it. In fact, there are times when life is pure pleasure.

****

We all claim we want to be happy and happiness must necessarily hold the experience of pleasure at its core. Happiness is not something we earn, nor is something we save. Happiness is always an immediate experience which comes to those who have the capacity to be themselves in the present moment.

While it is true that we can build a life which is more secure, more self-actualizing, more powerful and more loving, it is not possible to be happy unless we have the ability to exercise our innate joy of life. The ability to experience pleasure is a necessary component of happiness.

Pleasure, whether sexual pleasure, the pleasure of listening to beautiful music, the pleasure of eating a delicious meal, or taking the afternoon off and going for a walk on the beach, simply isn't on the agenda for a lot of modern women.

From time to time, we need to ask ourselves if we are having any fun? Or are we living a life which feels a lot like Super-woman with molting wings. In these time-pressured days, pleasure deserves top billing on the TO DO list of any woman on Wisdom's Path.

Recently, I was giving a talk on women's history to a group of women and I spoke about the first women in the United States who actually earned wages - the Lowell Mill girls. As I spoke of their long hours, I realized that many of the women in my audience were living lives with schedules which were as tight as those first female workers in the 1830s. The mill girls worked from six in the morning till ten at night with only three hours of breaks. They lived in boarding houses and had all their meals prepared for them. What does your schedule look like?

Lack of time is the reason most women give for not having more fun in their lives. "What good is it to drive downtown to go to the opera if you can't keep your eyes open for the last act?" my friend asked as we decided to cancel our subscriptions last year.

It is true that many women's lives are too busy. Young mothers who work are happy if they get back and forth to their jobs, get their housework done and the kids in bed with their homework done. Nevertheless, there are always choices and always ways to rearrange priorities.

When time for yourself is a priority, you will find ways to manage to find some. When giving yourself pleasure is a priority, you will attract fun people and fun events. There are always choices to make your life more fun, so open up more time and give yourself more pleasure.

Short hair is easier to get ready in the morning than long hair. Kids don't have to have home-made cookies to survive. You can listen to pleasant music tapes on the way to work instead of irritating talk shows. You can pick lunch companions who are a pleasure to be with. Think about spending that next raise on some housecleaning help or having the laundry done. Put yourself and pleasure on the list of priorities and you'll find new ways to enjoy life.

Time is a major issue, but there are several other more subterranean cultural concepts working against a woman's enjoyment of any pleasurable activity.

As a group, Americans have inherited a Puritan ethic which suspects any activity whose only apparent value is to give pleasure. Most girls got this Puritanical message and it was topped off by another message about girls needing to always be ladylike and well-behaved. So between being good enough and ladylike enough, a lot of us learned to suspect, or even deny, our capacity to have fun.

There is such a tendency to forego the moment and work toward some cumulative goal. We save our money for retirement and never find a way to take a vacation. We spend our Saturdays cleaning house and wish we could go to the Halloween Parade. Unconsciously, we are living out an ethic which is based on a belief that life is struggle. Those bumper stickers that say, "First you work hard, then you die," reflect one poisonous idea floating around in our society. Bumper stickers like that are examples of toxic thinking. Don't let your mind or your life be the local landfill!

Having too much fun is simply against the rules for a lot of us grown-up little girls, especially if it involves any kind of loud, boisterous or physical activity. Can you play? Do you know how to have fun? When you go to parties and they want to play charades do you want to run and hide?

Imagine yourself in a swimming pool tossing a ball back and forth. How noisy can you be? How loudly can you laugh? How funny can you look? Can you let go of the image of "good girl" long enough to enjoy yourself at a Saturday afternoon football game?

Ever noticed how much louder and more fun-loving a group of women can be when there are no men around? How many times have you been in a group of women who were telling stories and laughing and having a high old time and someone's husband walked into the kitchen and asked, "What are you girls laughing about?" The poor guy might as well be asking, "Did you hear the Bubonic Martians just landed?" The women stare at him, shift their posture and look sideways over his shoulder and say, "Oh nothing."

Do you think one reason why there's as much mistrust between men and women is that men suspect that women are somehow - <u>different</u> - when they are not around? One way to bridge the gender gap could be to begin to play more together. Men in the den watching football while the women are in the kitchen laughing about their families is only one model for suburban life. How about everyone in the living room once in a while, taking turns telling funny stories?

If you are in a committed relationship with another person, ask yourself what you can do to add fun and pleasure to that relationship. Couples who have fun together stay together - and that fun can be camping on the desert, going dancing every Friday night, or cooking gourmet dinners. Relationships don't have to be serious to be committed and they don't have to be a struggle to be healthy.

Pleasure comes in many different forms and pleasurable choices vary from woman to woman. Many women believe that their ability to experience pleasure in a sexual relationship is dependent upon their level of trust, of security, of feeling special, of feeling valued and loved. Often, they bring a large basket of validation needs to bed with them. The unspoken deal is that having sex with so-and-so will bring them the self-esteem, the sense of self-worth and self-love they need to be happy. Even the most committed relationships find that a heavy load.

Recently I attended a workshop where men and women were discussing sexual differences and the men claimed they wanted their partners to initiate sex more often. The women complained that men said that but they didn't really mean it. The men said that women had to risk rejection, just as they always did. The women were having a lot of trouble hearing that one. As I listened to all the rhetoric flying around the room, I realized what <u>hard work</u> the whole issue seemed to be for the participants who were clearly trying to nail down the rules so that they would risk less.

It is wiser to stop worrying about getting no-risk guarantees from your partner and concentrate on building your self-esteem high enough to have the courage to ask for what you want without feeling as though you put <u>everything about yourself</u> at risk. We can ask and not get when we know we are basically wonderful women who have enough self-validation to live healthy, fulfilling lives without a stamp of approval from someone else. That is not an impossible goal - that is something people who enjoy life have as an ordinary attribute.

Some women still see sex as too big a bargaining chip to ever let it go in simple pleasure. Their partners have to carry the trash out first and their partners also <u>always</u> have to make the initial overtures. A sexual relationship based on one person doing the other person a favor is not a lot of fun.

Our sexuality depends on the ability to give and receive pleasure. It is an exchange of energy and joy and love. Whether it is a lifetime commitment is not as important as whether there is mutual trust and agreement involved.

Developing the ability to enjoy life without attaching a lot of "shoulds" doesn't mean you have to always say yes. Saying yes should be a free and conscious choice, just as saying no is.

The pleasure principle, including sexual pleasure, is a life-affirming, life-enhancing principle. Life without pleasure would not suit us. We find pleasure in our own wonderful ways and as we know ourselves better, we are more and more comfortable in saying, "This is who I am. This is what suits me. This is what I want to do. This gives me pleasure."

Learning to give ourselves internal permission to have fun is a task on wisdom's path. We want to be whole women, with all our capacities intact, and among those capacities is the ability to experience pleasure. The joy of life is in accomplishment, in expression of our talents and in the giving of love. The experience of the joy of life is in this moment.

****

QUESTIONS

1. If I could add more pleasure to my life, what would I add?

2. What am I currently doing for myself that is pure pleasure?

3. How do I really feel about my sexuality?

4. Do I know how to have fun?

5. What is fun for me in my life right now?

AFFIRMATIONS

I deserve a wonderful life.

I enjoy my life.

I am a loving, sexual person.

I am having fun right now.

CHAPTER
TWENTY-SIX

WISE WOMEN
LET GO OF THE PAST

It is 1975. Jane is 42 years old. She is riding a bus in Mexico, traveling to the Guatemalan border to renew her papers once again. She has made this trip before but this time is different. This time she has been sober for four months.

Jane lets her eyes close as the bus winds down the steep hillsides and she remembers the very last time she was on this bus. She was so drunk she had to spend the night in the Tehuantepec Hotel.

That was the time she saw rats running along the walls of the room and wasn't sure whether they were really there or she had the d.t.'s. That was the time she lay with her head turned toward the wall, looking at the wide white holes in the blue plaster walls and tried to read her future in the markings of places that needed to be patched. That was the time she was so ashamed and sick that she seriously considered killing herself.

Jane realizes she is obsessing over the past and she sits up, reminding herself that she is now supposed to be living 24 hours at a time. She mumbles under her breath that the past is gone forever.

Jane has brought two prayer books on this trip. One is a small black book filled with affirmations and thoughts for each day. She rereads today's affirmation and then turns to her second prayer book - a translation of Jewish prayers. She opens the book to the prayer in which the writer says he is a parched tree whose roots have now found the blessed renewal of water. It is a poem written three thousand years ago by a desert dweller, but Jane understands it totally and completely. She, too, has found the blessed spring of renewal and her thirst is quenched.

Suddenly, it strikes her that she never has to drink again. She realizes that the past really is gone forever and that she does not have to repeat old behavior patterns, nor does she have to live in a state of perpetual repentance. She can simply live a good life.

Once again, she says, "The past is gone forever." This time, tears of relief and joy run down her face. She feels her heart open up and she feels such great relief that she knows she has truly changed. She will never be thirsty again.

****

One of the most important ideas in metaphysics is that we are always living in the moment. The past is truly gone forever and need not control our present or future if we can really let it go.

Once you get hold of the idea that your current thoughts are creating your future, it is not so difficult to understand why the past no longer needs to have any power over you.

Psychology has done a lot for our understanding of human motivation and human conditioning, but it is tragic when people accept vague psychological ideas that they will somehow always be limited by their early childhood conditioning. It is not only tragic, it is false.

When I was drinking, I felt guilty and ashamed because I was behaving in ways which did not fit my personal value system. When I stopped drinking, I chose to let the past go and make something of the remainder of my life, I was free to do that.

We are really as free as we can believe we are. It doesn't matter what has happened to you, what you have done, if you are willing to live in this wonderful moment, you can live a good life. I talk to women who have overcome all sorts of situations, histories and troubles. They are as free as they can imagine themselves to be. When they accept themselves as people who are living in this moment, they are all right. It doesn't matter who you are - you do not have to let the past control your life.

There are things that happen to people that influence them in negative ways. Even if they can't control the event, they can control their action and responses. The death of a loved one can create havoc in our lives for a while. We have a choice whether we will let that death color the rest of our days or not.

We all know elderly widows who blossom in their new freedom and spend their time with friends, traveling all over the world and doing good works. They had a choice whether to let the loss of their husbands mar the remainder of their days. They chose to control their lives.

It really doesn't matter what it is in your past which is haunting you. It need not do so. Make amends if you can. Don't repeat the mistakes. Help someone else. Move on. Live life. <u>The past is gone forever.</u>

Even a happy past can be a trap. To talk incessantly about your girlhood days on the plantation is to bore people away from you. No matter how popular you were in high school, it is over. Get out and get some friends in today's world. Learn the new dances, visit the new churches, meet some new people. Be a today person.

****

QUESTIONS

1. Are you controlled by the past?

2. What would you like to release?

3. What have you done recently that is new and different?

4. Do you talk a lot about your past marriage? Past childhood? Past boyfriends?

5. Do you have anyone from your past that you'd like to make amends to?

AFFIRMATIONS

The past is gone forever.

I am an now person living today's life.

I love my life now and I don't let the past stop me from having fun.

The past doesn't control me.

My future is in my present thoughts and actions. I love my future. I let go of my past.

I don't ever have to do_____ again. I live in the present moment.

CHAPTER
TWENTY-SEVEN

WISE WOMEN
COME IN ALL AGES

It is 1994. Jane is 61. She is sitting with another woman who is close to her age and they are laughing about the trouble they've seen, the places they've been and the fun they've had. They obviously feel good about themselves.

Each is writing books. Each is involved in a major new step up the career ladder and each is excited about the future. Jane's friend is telling a story about being on a radio talk show and grabbing the microphone away from the interviewer to say what she wants to say. Jane is applauding her brave action with laughter.

Suddenly, Jane's friend stops and asks, "Why didn't anyone tell us how much fun it would be to grow older?"

Jane nods her head. "Of course it's fun. You get to the place of freedom when you can honestly ask, "What can they do to me?""

"Maybe we should tell younger women," her friend suggests.

They nod and agree that they ought to get the message out.

****

We live in a society that is terrorized by the thought of aging. Women (and men) spend millions of dollars for products which they hope will make them appear younger. They monitor their conversation so they won't say words like <u>icebox</u> or <u>running board.</u> They pretend they don't remember when the Beatles first came to America and that they never heard of Edward R. Murrow. Behind this desperate coverup is an assumption that younger is better.

Younger has certain advantages. When you are young, you have a lot of time in which to make choices, decisions, and even mistakes. You also have the beauty that comes from the natural blush of youth. You can be very happy when you are young if you are emotionally able and willing to deal with the myriad choices, unlimited opportunity and challenges that come with defining yourself.

The middle years are also wonderful. Most of us love the excitement of climbing the career ladder, of being involved parents, of having committed relationships and of dealing with all the <u>householder</u> issues that come in the middle. You can be very happy with the intense here-and-now qualities of the middle years if you are emotionally able and willing to deal with the challenges of relationships, children, ambitious colleagues, civic responsibilities and resolving that mid-life crisis.

Here's the surprising news! The older years are a great big wonderful pay-off for all the earlier work you've done. To the extent that you can accept aging as natural and stop hating the image you see in the mirror, you can have more fun and love life more than ever. You just have to be wise enough to live life in the present, not hold onto the past out of fear of the future.

Living in the here and now is really important at any age. It is absolutely essential after fifty. Sure, you can have plastic surgery and you can stay lean and trim. You can dress well and you can take care of your appearance. You can dye your hair and you can look wonderful. That's all great if it leads to a happier life.

What's not great is to deny yourself and who you really are. Being able to accept the woman in the mirror is crucial at any age. At no time is it more crucial than in the later years. It takes courage to step out and be in charge of your life and in some ways, it takes more courage when you are over fifty and living in a society which constantly says, "Young is good."

Young is young. Middle is middle and old is old. It's all good if we allow it to be. The best time is the one we are in because it is the only time in which to be happy. One absolute ingredient of wisdom is to understand this basic fact - the only time in which you can be happy is now.

I wasted a great deal of my younger years by wanting to be someone I was not and wanting to be in a place I was not and most of all - wanting to be in a time I was not. I was so future-oriented that I simply didn't know what people were talking about when they said we should live in the here and now.

Living in the here and now means exactly that. It is the key to happiness at any age. Older people who are active and involved in life are living in the here and now. Those who are living in the past are only half alive and those who are living in fear of the future are less than half alive.

Actually, nearly everyone gets emotional payoffs just for surviving to the point of "that certain age." One must begin to shed a lot of the earlier concerns because life forces you to do so. If you can shed the foolishness with good grace and laughter, life gets to be even more fun. I can remember when I was teaching school in four-inch heels laughing about "little old ladies in tennis shoes." The joke was on me! I never got to be a little old lady, but Birkenstocks are certainly my footwear of choice these days.

As one matures, whether at 16, 36, 56 or 86, one quite naturally achieves a place in consciousness where one is really ready to make independent life choices.

Those choices can include wearing tennis shoes and they can also include giving your money to favorite charities. What seems like foolishness or willfulness to older people's children is often the simple exercising of independent choice.

Growing older almost has to lead to a certain amount of maturity and happiness. There are plenty of studies which support the fact that most older women consider themselves "very happy," and if we are wise, we will acknowledge that happiness when we find it in our older friends and ourselves. There is absolutely no reason to buy into the belief that you fall off the edge of the earth on your 50th birthday.

Let's remember, happiness at any age depends on wisdom. Physical maturity doesn't always bring emotional maturity. Wisdom isn't an absolute pay-off for growing older. We all know people walking around in 70-year-old bodies who are still dealing with the same issues and emotions they were attempting to deal with at 16. Dirty old men are just teenagers in disguise. Silly old women who spend their days in unhappy gossip, wishing they could find just one more boyfriend, are living in a time warp.

This culture has a lot of work to do on our attitudes toward aging and I note that there is some interest in doing the work now that the baby boomers are hitting fifty. It is to the advantage of every woman, no matter what her current age is, to become involved in the general shift in thinking about what aging means. No matter how old we are now, we will one day be older.

We can help prepare ourselves for a great aging process if we expand our ability to accept older people into our current lives. Why not make it a point to make a friend or two who is outside of your particular age group? Your church, your organizations and your workplace offer opportunities to meet people who are younger and older than you are. Why not extend your horizons to include people of different ages? You will certainly learn something and you will also enjoy a new friend.

Begin to think of aging in new ways. Anticipate the freedom it will bring. Anticipate the fun you will have with all that extra time and all those new choices. When your hair is white it will take dye really well and you can make it a hobby to change your hair color every week if you want to. Or you can finally begin to paint the paintings you've always dreamed of creating. You can join the Peace Corps. You can volunteer at schools in the ghetto. You can make wonderful new choices from the viewpoint of all your wonderful wisdom.

The pay-offs for growing older are somewhat secret in our society, partly because they don't fit into Madison Avenue's sales pitches. But the pay-offs are there and you can begin to notice them. Expand your horizons, expand your ideas about what life can offer at any age.

Some of the delight I have found in life after 50 has been in the activity of grand-parenting. Those charming little ones who come to visit are fun to play with, great to spoil, and treasures to have in your life. What's more, the responsibility of being a grandparent is much less than being a parent. You can send them home when they give you trouble.

Another delightful thing about being an older woman is that life experience has already given you many opportunities to express courage, express love, and express joy. Those positive expressions of your particular brand of wisdom are cumulative in effect. Look around at the faces of older people who are enjoying life and see how beautiful they really are.

****

QUESTIONS

1. How do you really feel about aging?

2. What would you like to change about your beliefs about your current age?

3. What do you expect the benefits of aging to be?

4. What does "ageless" mean to you.

5. What older (than you) women do you find beautiful. Why?

AFFIRMATIONS

Life is wonderful!

I am the perfect age right now!

I love my life right now!

I am growing wiser each day.

CHAPTER
TWENTY-EIGHT

WISE WOMEN
COME IN ALL SIZES

It is 1978. Jane is 44 years old. She is in her yoga class and she is the fattest person in the room. The class is moving from one posture to another and Jane is doing her own version of the bends and stretches. She is wearing a bright green leotard and she is feeling all right about being in the class.

Her teacher decides it is time to do one of their special exercises and everyone needs to find a partner. The teacher tells Richard to work with Jane and Jane wishes she could go home early. The last time she had Richard for a partner he told her she was surprisingly limber for a fat person. She can still remember the condescension in his voice.

Jane didn't much like Richard before that. Now she really doesn't like him. What's more, this exercise is more than simple physical exercise. The teacher explains that this is an exercise in mirroring. Jane realizes she is going to have to stand and stare into Richard's eyes the whole time.

She and Richard stand opposite each other and move in unison. It is a non-verbal process and they must look into each other's eyes to pick up the clues about what they will do next. Each must stay with the other and there can be no leader, everything has to be done by non-verbal agreement.

Even thinking about looking into Richard's eyes makes Jane feel uncomfortable. She believes he is very judgmental about her weight and she believes he is too bossy to be a good silent partner. Nevertheless, she does as she is told.

She is surprised to discover that Richard has deep blue eyes and it is surprisingly easy to focus on them. She tries very hard to focus on the exercise and keep her own critical nature out of the way. It is easier than she expected.

She and Richard find they do very well as long as they are in quiet communication. By the time the five minute mirroring exercise is over, she knows she has learned to know Richard in an entirely different way. She will not let his conversation throw her off guard any longer. She now knows that she and Richard are connected at the level of Truth. They are both children of God and they are much more alike than different. Richard is no longer "the other."

Later that day, it occurs to her that she feared Richard would condemn her for her weight, but it is really her own self-condemnation which is the problem. She doesn't need to spend much time with Richard, but she has to live with herself. She doesn't need his approval, but she needs her own self-love in order to be a happy person.

She realizes that what Richard thinks about her is none of her business - that the key is what she thinks about herself. She also realizes that she has projected a lot of critical stuff onto Richard when he probably could care less. She decides to try and keep the feeling of closeness she has developed through the exercise. She decides she doesn't have to think of him as "the other." For that matter, she is probably more like Richard than any other person in that class. Both of them would be better off if they could drop the verbal defenses and criticism and simply focus on being here now. She and Richard have a lot in common.

****

People are very different from each other in many ways, including body size. Nowhere is the idealized image of what we are "supposed to be" as damaging to women as in our relationships to our own bodies. Your body size may not fit those idealized images, but that doesn't mean you are doomed to unhappiness. Nor does it mean that your body size is wrong.

If you look at historical photographs you will discover that body size is as trendy as shoes or corsets. Right now, the trend is toward very lean bodies and not all of us fit those modern specifications.

The range of acceptable body weight has shrunk drastically in the last thirty years - possibly in response to the medium of television and its predilection to put twenty pounds on all of the people who are on the screen. Perhaps professional beauties have to diet to make money, but do the rest of us really want to walk around looking that thin?

The messages are very confusing and discouraging. On the one hand, Americans spend more on diet products than ever and are gaining weight. On the other hand, we are told we must be thin to be healthy but that dieting can be very dangerous and doesn't work permanently anyway. I suggest you consult your doctor for a realistic appraisal of your particular ideal weight.

The point is not how much we weigh but how well we live. Much of the idealization of physical appearance has only served to make women feel that here is another area where they simply can't measure up to the approved standards.

Even more insidious than idealizing a particular weight is the tendency to postpone life until we reach that desired goal. We have all seen beautiful, healthy women obsess over the ten or twenty pounds they wanted to lose. They won't go to the beach. They won't go anywhere because they don't want to spend money on clothes at their "fat weight." They prefer to sit home until they get into those "thin clothes" in their closets. We all know women who have nothing to wear and also have closets full of clothes they've outgrown.

Over the years as I have become a fat woman, I have learned some things about body weight and body size which I'd like to share. My struggles to understand and accept my weight have not produced a significant weight loss as yet, but they have produced some special wisdom about how to love and accept yourself at any size.

First of all, happiness does not depend on body size. Losing weight does not guarantee that you will be happy and even if you are happy, you may not lose weight. Separate the two ideas in your mind and focus on knowing yourself and your own motivations.

For years I have been reading junk about the connection between size and mental health - especially the connection between size and depression. While I will grant you that many overweight women are depressed about their weight, that is the only connection I have ever really been able to see substantiated.

Wearing a size 10 dress may be your ultimate goal and you can probably achieve that if you are willing to take the necessary steps, but don't make the mistake of delaying life until you can fit into that white pants suit. Happiness is a state of mind which is induced by a series of conscious choices, it is never dependent on an outside condition.

If you are planning to lose weight go ahead and find a plan of diet and exercise which seems sensible and follow it. Don't obsess out loud about your struggles or about your successes. No one wants to hear it. And do your fat friends a favor and leave them alone. They'll make their own decisions in their own time.

There are several metaphysical books and tapes on weight loss which are based on the idea that you can love yourself slim. In theory, if one could learn to love oneself enough, one could drop the weight easily and never pick it up. I believe they contain truth and can be very, very useful.

The trick is to love yourself in advance of regaining that slim figure. Being overweight offers many opportunities not to love oneself and so it is a challenging process. Loving oneself while fat is a wonderful achievement in this society. There are few other areas of modern life where people feel as free to be judgmental and critical as in the area of excess weight.

Food has replaced sex as the national sin. Listen to conversation at a ladies lunch and notice how often the word "sinful" comes up around the dessert table.

Despite our Puritanical attitudes, you can learn to love yourself no matter what your body size. You simply have to be willing to break out of the stereotypes which surround you and move into a self-reliant attitude toward life.

Remember that every choice you make sends a message to the Universe and to the world around you. Both Universal Mind and the companions you meet along life's journey will respond to your message. If you are miserable over your weight and your consistent message is "I am miserable," you will receive support to keep that message in place. If you put yourself together in such a way that your message is, "I am wonderful," you will find that the world thinks so as well.

Here are some actions you can take which will help you love yourself. Dress well in stylish, youthful clothing. If you have to spend a little more, tell yourself you are worth it and spend it. Don't fall into the trap of believing that you're supposed to look as if you are in mourning if you are over a size fourteen. Remember that you want to be noticed and admired. While it is all right to choose clothes which make you appear slimmer, you're not buying camouflage. You're buying a statement about the beautiful you.

Pay particular attention to your grooming. Make sure your hair and nails are well designed and kept up. Just because you are overweight, don't think that there is nothing you can do about your appearance. Fat doesn't have to be connected to sloppy. Think about some of the wonderful women you know who are in public life who are more than a size ten. Barbara Bush is great-looking. So is singer Marilyn Horn. Madeline Albright, the United States Ambassador to the United Nations, always finds time to have beautiful grooming and so can you.

Watch your shoes, purses and stockings. Make sure your shoes are sturdy enough to hold your weight well. And make sure they are polished and mended. Keep your purses and jewelry in proper proportion. All and all, make sure you look really well cared for. Keep your makeup simple and fresh. Smile a lot.

Exercise often at your own pace. Take care of yourself physically and eat as well as you can, sleep well and have fun. Never turn down a fun activity because you think you'd look or feel silly doing it. You have a right to go dancing even if you wear a size 22. You have a right to enjoy the beach in a size 18 swimsuit. You are a perfectly wonderful person and you have a right to have fun.

Stay out of guilt! If you eat something that you didn't plan to eat, throw away the wrapper and get on with your life. Continue to send a consistent message to the Universe which says, "I am wonderful."

The better you know yourself, the happier you will be. The better you know yourself, the better your chances of achieving a body weight which makes sense for you. One successful woman I know tells herself she is doing a good job if she loses a pound. She consistently tells herself she only needs to lose one pound. That way, she keeps her desired weight in view, one pound at a time.

226

If you are really interested in losing weight, join a support group which will help you do it. Choose one that focuses on making healthy and independent food choices.

Why not keep an I AM LOVE Journal in which you record your successes and your thoughts? The primary purpose is self-exploration, but the secondary purpose can be to isolate some of the old beliefs and release them.

Through learning to know yourself better, you may discover that you are holding on to weight in order to stay out of destructive relationships. You can learn to trust yourself to make wise choices. Or you may learn that you are holding on to weight because it doesn't really bother you and you're tired of dieting. You can decide on a new and more sensible weight for yourself.

Accepting and loving yourself at your current body size and weight puts you in a powerful place - a place where you are free to make intelligent, self-fulfilling choices. Wisdom has no particular package that it comes in and Wise Women come in all sizes and shapes.

****

QUESTIONS

1. How do you feel about your body weight and size right now?

2. How would you like to change your feelings about yourself?

3. Are there changes you would like to make in your body weight and size?

4. Do you consider yourself well-groomed now?

5. How might you change your choices on clothes and grooming?

AFFIRMATIONS

I am a beautiful woman.

I am a perfectly wonderful woman who moves with grace and ease.

I am lithe and flexible and youthful and joyful.

I am strong and healthy and full of joy.

I am graceful and delightful to look at.

I enjoy my body and I appreciate the way it moves.

CHAPTER
TWENTY-NINE

WISE WOMEN ARE
IN PROCESS

It is 1994. Jane is 61 years old. She is working on a book which will tell some of her life story. As she begins to write, she <u>notices</u> that she has problems with procrastination, self-criticism and inarticulateness.

What's more, she has the same nightmare twice and she hasn't had nightmares in years. In both dreams, her mother is very, very angry at her for telling the family secrets. She realizes that she is making yet another step out of the original boundaries which were drawn for her. She notices that she has no intention of turning back. She is wise enough to know that a little resistance is simply that - a little resistance.

As the book progresses, she begins to hear the voice of her colleagues in her ear. She especially hears male voices condemning the book because of its very nature. She accepts complete responsibility for those voices. They are her voices. No one is saying anything to her except what she is allowing her own internal voices to say.

She begins to replace the critical voices with an interior monologue which focusses on her reasons for writing the book and what she hopes to accomplish. She is wise enough to know she doesn't have to please everybody.

It is enough if she writes an honest, loving book. It is enough if some women find the courage, the strength and the wisdom to be more self-reliant in their own lives. It is enough that she had a vision and she acted on that vision.

When she thinks that she has no business writing about wisdom - that there is much she still doesn't know - she is wise enough to accept that she is <u>in process.</u> There will never be a time when everything will be perfectly in place, there will never be a time when she has all the answers. She is wise enough to know that sharing is important and she has chosen to share. It is enough.

****

Self-exploration still does not come easily to a woman who decides to discover herself, but every year we have a few more models of success. We are inventing ourselves, and thereby inventing our world - and it promises to be a very wonderful world.

Right now, in this very moment, every woman I know has a keener sense of self than she has ever had before. More women are speaking up. More women are saying, "This is how it was for me, but this is not the way I want it for my daughter."

In the early sixties, when I really began trying to understand myself and my world, there were very few books which offered female models for inner exploration. Our heroines in books were charming and dependent women such as the second wife in *Rebecca* or hussies such as Amber in *Forever Amber*. Not much in the way of role models there.

No one ever asked you which women you admired in those days. The acceptable models were Jackie Kennedy and Grace Kelly. If you were a nice girl, you aimed to be like one of those two. I wanted something else - I wanted the kind of authenticity I knew was possible, even though I didn't know how to get it.

Some of us found in the interior monologues of Doris Lessing and Anias Nin a kind of authenticity. I enjoyed them both, but their lives seemed very privileged and intellectual. I was always conscious of my lower-class beginnings and in order to be a whole person, I didn't want to deny the great common sense I'd learned from the ordinary women I'd known as a child.

Ordinary lives of ordinary women simply didn't get written in ways that seemed authentic or useful. I was a great reader and I loved all kinds of books, especially novels, but I don't remember ever finding a heroine who I felt close to as I read. I might have wished I were more like Becky Sharp or Emma Bovary, but I wasn't.

I wasn't the only one who felt out of step and invisible. Most women were hungry to know more about themselves and each other but we didn't really know what questions to ask or to know how we could talk about our own doubts and dreams. There weren't a lot of role models.

I lived near UCLA and Anais Nin was a visiting author so I went once to listen to her speak, but I simply could not hear her because she was wearing a cape and that struck me as a dishonest pose. She seemed too dramatic, too intellectual and too precious to have much to say that I could hear. Besides, I had once heard that she hocked her typewriter to feed Henry Miller. What kind of a role model was a woman who would hock her typewriter for a man? She did not suit me.

I also went to hear Margaret Mead, not because I was particularly interested in anthropology, but because she had made it in a man's world. I couldn't get in the door because the huge lecture hall was packed with women who were searching for the same model of authenticity.

The arts were my lifeline, but most artists were men. Beautiful women could act but only men wrote, directed and produced movies. Men were painters and classical musicians. Men were jazz musicians. The only authentic women's voices were singers such as Billie Holliday, Nina Simone and Dinah Washington.

I loved traditional jazz and I loved the blues singers - male and female - and I loved the rough, unpolished voices of the oldest and best. Leadbelly was my hero. Bessie Smith was a marvel. I had my favorite songs and they usually reflected a kind of down-home wisdom which I admired. Whether the lyrics said, *Ain't Nobody's Business If I Do* or *Wild Women Don't Worry, Wild Women Don't Sing The Blues*, I found a core of wisdom in the free and independent stance of these wonderful women. I found role models in those songs.

Right about then, *The Feminine Mystique* announced the rise of women's liberation. I was interested but I didn't really need or want political solutions. I needed to acquire a deeper understanding of who I was and what I wanted. I didn't want to live the role of activist or victim. I wanted to love and be loved. I needed to learn to accept and love myself. I needed to accept responsibility for making a good life. I needed the ideas that metaphysics offered.

Gradually, I began to get the idea that I was connected to life at a cosmic level. I had small and then greater experiences which made me suspect that my life was somehow connected to the universal, organic, holistic health of the world.

When I undertook the search for self, I was a wild woman. I was frantic with my sense of not knowing myself and I was hysterical because I thought the only power I has was my fading sex appeal. Even as I was playing out a combination of Ophelia, Sadie Thompson and Ernest Hemingway, I had some sense that if I figured myself out, I could help others.

In those days, I could not have articulated the possibility that I was a microcosm in the macrocosm of life. Nor could I have been able to say that I was a mystic or that I sensed a mystical connection with the world and with other travelers on the Spaceship Earth. All I really knew was that I needed to find some way to get a hold on life which had some meaning.

What happens to wild women? Not all of them die before the last reel. Some of them switch an LD to SE and become wise. My personal journey was a search for self that involved a lot of risk but it was worth the trip. What would have happened if I had played it safe? What happens to old wooden boats which just sit around in the harbor? They collect barnacles and eventually they sink beneath the surface.

Two husbands dead. One child in college and not coming home. The game plan given me by society hadn't worked at all. So I set out to discover myself. Then I changed the lyrics I was singing to suit my new understanding of life.

The title of this book is *Wise Woman Don't Worry, Wise Women Don't Sing The Blues.* I make the claim that I have become a wise woman. Part of my wisdom is the sure and certain knowledge that it is good to offer what you can give with love.

I believe you can also claim to be a Wise Woman if you are willing to take a look at new possibilities and opportunities to be whole, independent and loving. Won't you join me in making the circle wider?

****

QUESTIONS

1. How do you want to use this book?

2. Would you like to write your own life story?

3. Would you like to set up a consciousness-raising group called Wise Women?

4. Would you like to write the author a letter and tell her what you think about her ideas?

5. Would you like to give this book to a friend?

AFFIRMATIONS

I am a Wise Woman.

I love myself.

I listen to my inner wisdom and follow my inner guidance.

I am self-reliant.

I manage my time and money well.

I manage my life well.

My conversation is interesting and cheerful.

I am very optimistic about my life.

All is well - God and I are One.

CHAPTER
THIRTY

AFFIRMATIVE PRAYER

Affirmative prayer or spiritual mind treatment is a method of sending a message to the Universal Mind which is direct, clear and focussed. It can be used to change any area of your life.

You can learn to do affirmative prayer on your own, and there are some excellent books which teach the techniques. The simplest explanation I have seen is in my workbook, *Science of Mind Skills*. The most thorough and authoritative is *How To Use Science of Mind* by Dr. Ernest Holmes. *Treat Yourself To Life* by Dr. Raymond Charles Barker is also very useful.

You will do much better if you can find a good class where a teacher can monitor your progress and make suggestions. The best place to learn the art of affirmative prayer is in metaphysical church classes because you get a chance to practice with other students and you also have an experienced guide.

The most important points in using affirmative prayer include getting to the place in your own mind where you <u>know</u> that what you are claiming is already in the works for you. Sometimes that is an easy, quick process. Sometimes it takes a while but it is always worth the effort.

Remember at all times that you are working with an unlimited Power For Good and that there is no need to plea bargain, manipulate or beg. State your claim and accept it mentally and then let it go.

The following affirmative prayers can be used by anyone who wants to use them. Quite a few of them were first published in *Creative Thought Magazine*. I suggest you select the one or two you want to use and read them out loud to yourself one or two times a day until you are really able to see, feel, touch and accept the vision you have established.

It is the nature of the Universal Mind to respond to any clear cut, definite mental vision which you hold. These affirmative prayers are short cuts in the process of getting what you want. They will work to the extent that you can believe you deserve the good you desire and you can accept that good into your life.

Publishers and literary gents once told me I could never make a success writing about Chinese people. I thought of that the day I stood before the King of Sweden to receive the Nobel Prize.

Pearl Buck

I AM SELF-CONFIDENT

The nature of God is Creative Intelligence and my nature is also creative and intelligent. I use my God-given intelligence to direct my life experience.

I am self-confident. I choose to live a successful life and I choose positive thoughts.

I understand that prevailing belief patterns can be changed and that I can make new choices. I think optimistically.

Where there may have been fear, I now think courageously. I am energetic, optimistic and creative. I take appropriate actions each day.

Gently, without self-condemnation, I move my mind into the habit of positive thinking. I choose to express the Truth that sets me free. I choose to live my life from the highest attitude I can now envision and I allow that vision to constantly expand and elevate.

I release these words with gratitude and joy, confident that Creative Intelligence responds immediately to my wonderful decision to live life positively. I am confident that I am attracting the best. I let go and let God.

The universe is made up of pure energy, the nature of which is to move and flow. The nature of life is constant change, constant flux. When we understand this, we turn into its rhythm and we are able to give and receive freely knowing that we never really lose anything, but constantly gain.

Shakti Gawain

I AM RENEWED

Infinite Intelligence creates all and I rely on Infinite Intelligence to renew and recreate me. I rest in the love of God, letting God support me, guide me and heal me. I am renewed.

No matter what kind of challenges I meet this day, I rely on the security, the reliability and the love which I know is there in my ever present support from Infinite Love.

I trust life. I trust the process of growth and change. I trust love. I trust myself and my ability to handle life. I trust that all is well and that there is nothing to fear or regret.

I know that at the level of God's Truth, I am all right. There is nothing I need to change in order to be loved by God. God knows me as perfect, whole and complete. All is well and I rest in that beautiful knowledge. I am all right the way I am. I am the Beloved.

You were not made for failure, no matter who you are, nor how much you know, nor what anyone has told you. God is your prosperity. God, the Most High, is your defense. God, the Absolute Good, is your friend.

Emma Curtis Hopkins

I ACCEPT SUCCESS

I know that there is only One Power in my life and that power is God Power. I now rely completely on God as I express total success.

As I make my daily decisions, I rely on God for guidance. As I go about my daily tasks, I know God supports me. As I dream my dreams and make my plans, I know that God is able and willing to bring into form the highest vision I can accept for my self.

I accept health. I accept happiness. I accept prosperity. I accept love. I accept a deeper knowledge of my relationship to God. I accept the very best for myself.

There is no thought of failure in my mind. There is only the complete acceptance of success. As I can accept, so it is done.

This day, I am filled with gratitude for the wonderful success which is now mine. And so it is.

We all like people who do things even if we only see their faces on a cigar-box lid.

Willa Cather

I ACCEPT MY POWER

God is One and I am one with God. I see and feel this clearly as I go about my daily activities. I have the power to accomplish much. I have the power to be happy, healthy, wealthy and wise. I do not need to beg or whine or supplicate, I simply need to know that my connection with God empowers my life.

As God is Creative Process and I am made in the image and likeness of God, I understand that I too, am in the process of creating. My thoughts are always sending joyful, expectant messages to God. I am creating a wonderful world for myself.

My thoughts which create my marvelous mental atmosphere, are always focussed on the good I experience and expect to experience. I let all belief in evil, in disappointment, in delay or in difficulty drop away from my mind. I focus on the best because I expect the best. The best comes to me quickly and easily because there is no impediment in my mind to the working of spiritual law.

My connection to God is creating the very best in my world and I rejoice that this is so and so it is.

Relationships are mirrors of ourselves.

Louise Hay

I ATTRACT LOVE

God is Love and love is the action of God. Since I live, move and have my life in God, I too am love and my loving actions are a way of knowing God.

I now choose to be more loving and to attract more love into my life. Love is the center of my life. It resides in my heart and radiates out in all directions. My thoughts are loving thoughts, my words are loving words and my actions are loving actions. I send a steady signal of love to the Universe.

Of the many attributes of God, love is the most dear to me, because it is the healing balm in my life.

As I make a conscious choice to exemplify love this day, I know that my life will be immediately filled with more than ever before. I shall attract new people into my life. I shall discover new depths of love in current friends and family.

Since love is my nature, I attract more and more love to me. Since love begets love, I see my self as I truly am. I am a radiant being of love, giving off a strong pulse of love and accepting a stronger pulse of love back. I am constantly expanding and deepening my loving nature. And so it is.

I had a pleasant time with my mind for it was happy.

Louisa Mae Alcott

I HAVE DECIDED TO BE HAPPY

Mind is Creative Process and Mind is all-intelligent. I now give direct focus to Mind as I make the definite decision to be happy.

I have decided to be happy. This happiness includes excellent health, great relationships, freedom from worry, financial balance and creative expression.

I expect the Universe to reveal new ideas to me so that my decision can be effectively implemented. I am open and receptive to newness and change. I am open and receptive to the gifts of Creative Intelligence. I am willing to work at an intuitive and responsive level as I make God my partner in my happiness decision.

I know that guidance is there because I have decided to listen for it. I know that solutions are present because I have decided to accept them. I know that happiness is here because I have decided to express it.

My total reliance on God brings the decision to be happy into being with ease, speed and imaginative surprises. I am ready for the best! I let go and let God. And so it is.

Truth is the unchangeable part of me.

Louise Hay

I HANDLE CHANGE WELL

God is constantly creating new conditions, new events and new experiences in my life and I know that I can always choose to benefit and enjoy change.

While it may not be immediately apparent, I understand that any challenge is an opportunity for growth and that any change is a natural progression of life. I am willing and able to adjust to new events, new circumstances and new conditions.

I greet change with absolute faith in the goodness of life. I handle surprises with calm acceptance that change is inevitable. I am serene and I accept that which I cannot change with a peaceful mind. I also have the courage to pursue my goals and adjust my life strategy so that I can live a prosperous, joyful life.

I waste no time feeling sorry for myself. I am never overwhelmed by change. I am always centered in the truth of God's love for me. I am always willing to greet changing conditions with an optimistic frame of mind. I am an active and joyful participant in life. And so it is.

Would I wish to be "young" again? No, for I have learned too much to wish to lose it. I am a far more valuable person than I was 50 years ago, or 40 years ago, or 30, 20 or even 10. I have learned so much since I was 70. I believe I can honestly say that I have learned more in the last 10 years than I learned in any previous decade.

Pearl Buck on her 80th birthday

I AM IN PROCESS

I understand that the nature of life is change and that my nature is to expand in intelligence, beauty and wisdom each day. I am never old, but I am accumulating wisdom and strength of purpose as I move along life's pathway.

I love my life and I love the fact that I am always opening up to new ideas, new experiences, new learning and new joys. At every age, I am all ages for I am in tune with the Infinite.

I am in process and that means that I am never finished and I am always growing better and better. It is a wonderful place to be - in process!

I give up all fear of aging. I let go of all perfectionism. I allow my life to be joyous, free and self-actualizing. Each day I rejoice that my life is a wonderful life. And so it is.

Truth is the nursing mother of genius.

Margaret Fuller

I SPEAK OUT

I know that my life is supported by Truth and that I am able to speak my truth with clarity, and decision. I speak out with joy, energy and intelligence.

I accept my God-given right to speak up and to speak out. I have much to contribute to the world and I want to share. I am willing to do what I need to do, know what I need to know to release all impediments to speaking freely.

I release all fear. I release all need to compromise in order to please. I release all self-doubt and all hesitancy. I speak the thoughts I have to say with ease, wit, grace, and with a fine intelligence.

My energy is clear and simple. I do not need to propel my courage by anger - I am able to speak with love. I do not need to introduce my words with an apology - my life is not an apology.

I am an effective communicator. I say what I think in a way people can hear it. I listen and reconsider but I am not bullied by vehemence. I am situated in truth and I speak definitely.

All is well. My words are well received and my value is fulfilled. I release these words with gratitude for the results. And so it is.

I want, by understanding myself, to understand others. I want to be all that I am capable of becoming ... This all sounds very strenuous and serious. But now that I have wrestled with it, it's no longer so. I feel happy - deep down. <u>All is well.</u>

Katherine Mansfield

I AM WISE

As I move into wisdom, I understand that I am eternally connected to my Source - God. I also understand that the answers to all my questions are to be found within me and that my life is a spiritual journey along Wisdom's Path.

I accept the challenge of knowing myself. I accept the delight of exploring my inner world. I accept the necessity to love myself. I accept myself - exactly as I am - right in this moment.

I am delighted to be me. I am delighted to live the life I am living. I am delighted that I have come far enough along Wisdom's Path to be able and willing to change some things and accept the others.

I love myself. I love my surroundings. I love my dear circle of friends and family. I love my life. The love that I feel is the proof of the wisdom I have gained.

I am Love. I am happy. I am a Wise Woman.

I release these words knowing they are planted in fertile soil, take root, grow and flower. And so it is.

Life is a banquet...

Auntie Mame

TREATMENT FOR RICHES

God is everywhere, spilling out abundance because abundance is the nature of God. As there are hundreds of billions of grains of sand and hundreds of billions of leaves of grass, there are billions of ideas which bring me happiness and riches.

I accept happiness as part of the abundance of the Universe. I accept riches as a part of that happiness. I accept a life of peace and plenty as a part of the Divine Plan.

I am ready to accept a great deal of wealth and a great deal of happiness. I know that there is enough to go around and that I am entitled to enjoy the very best that life has to offer. I am glad to be alive and my gladness manifests as financial freedom.

As there are fish in the sea, birds in the sky, sand on the beaches, flowers in the fields, there are dollars in my pockets. I can never be without because I am part of this abundant Universe. And so it is!

WISE WOMAN CREDO

1. Wise Women don't blame others.

2. Wise Women aren't victims.

3. Wise Women don't criticize others.

4. Wise Women don't worry.

5. Wise Women don't sing the blues.

BASIC METAPHYSICAL IDEAS

1. There is a Power For Good working in our lives now.

2. We are in contact with and actually direct this Power For Good through our thoughts and beliefs.

3. Much of the negative in our lives comes from unconscious behaviors which are based on outworn, unnecessary ideas and beliefs. We can make a choice to change behavior when we become conscious of how those activities no longer fit our beliefs.

4. Life is a spiritual journey and we are all in the process of self discovery.

5. Each of us has access to Universal Power. In that way, we are each very powerful.

6. When we blame others for our misery, we are actually misusing our power. We give our power away or fail to claim what is rightly ours.

7. Everyone has the right and the ability to be loved, to be happy, to be healthy, to be wealthy and to be wise. As we learn new skills, discover our inner worth, and accept our God-given ability to use Universal Power, we move in the direction of happiness, healthfulness, wealth and wisdom.

8. Our thoughts and attitudes are powerful messages to the Universe and to each other. We create a mental atmosphere through our thoughts; our mental atmosphere draws experiences, events and circumstances to us. As we change our thinking, our mental atmosphere changes and we attract new people, places and things.

9. Our relationships are a reflection of what we believe abut ourselves. For instance, if I believe someone is cruel to me, that may reflect a belief in powerlessness or a belief that I deserve punishment (or any number of other beliefs).

10. There is no *blame* in metaphysics. We are all on a pathway toward understanding the nature of Life as Love. We don't have to blame the victim, nor do we have to analyze the criminal. We simply move away into a new experience.

SUGGESTED BIBLIOGRAPHY
FOR FURTHER READING

You can find most of these books in metaphysical bookstores.

Barker, Raymond Charles. *Treat Yourself to Life.* Putnam, $9.95. Concise and well-written explanation of spiritual mind treatment (affirmative prayer) by one of New Thought's master writers.

Barker, Raymond Charles. *Power of Decision.* Putnam, 0-399516749 $9.95. He writes like an English teacher's dream. Each paragraph has a topic sentence and the ideas will surely move you into action. A must!

Claypool, Jane. *Science of Mind Skills.* Cornucopia Press, 0-9643948-0-4 $14.95. Metaphysical concepts explained so simply you'll be glad you read it first. Contains many excellent skill builders, affirmations and treatments.

Gawain, Shakti. *Creative Visualization.* Bantam, 0-553-24247-8 $3.95. This book tells you how to use your imagination to create a better life. Excellent for everyone - especially people who don't want to deal with references to God. Secular.

Goldberg, Natalie. *Writing Down The Bones - Freeing The Writer Within.* Shambala Press, 0-87773-375-9 $10.00.

I think this is the best of the new crop of writing books because Goldberg is an excellent writer and a serious practitioner of Zen.

Grayson, Stewart. *Ten Demandments of Prosperity.* Putnam, 0-399-550055-4 $11.95. Grayson is a long-time minister of Religious Science in New York City. He covers every aspect of prosperity teaching very thoroughly. More complicated than some prosperity books and also more helpful.

Groves, Dawn. *Meditation For Busy People.* New World Library, 1-880032-02-3 $10.95. Modern, no-nonsense introduction to meditation. I especially liked the section on how to choose a meditation teacher and think the advice applies to spiritual teachers in general.

Hay, Louise L. *You Can Heal Your Life.* Hay House, 0937611-01-8 $12.00. All her books are excellent but this is the most general. Her clear writing style and modern approach have done a lot to put metaphysical healing into the general public's awareness. Easy to follow. Easy to read.

Ponder, Catherine. *Dynamic Laws of Prosperity.* DeVorss, 0-875161-6 $11.95. This writer has many books on prosperity and they were the best available for a long time. Still contain many valuable ideas although their style is a bit old fashioned. Easy to read.

Rayser, V. Fred. *Seven Secrets For Getting What You Want.* Winged Lion Press,, 09159220022 $6.95. Little known, very simple and useful book.

Richelieu, Frank. *Art of Being Yourself: Discover Who You Are and Learn How To Live.* Science of Mind Books, 0-917489-15-9 $12.95. Popular speaker and minister, Dr. Frank of Redondo Beach gives some excellent tips on working with the spiritual laws to come into your own powerful truth.

Ross, Ruth. *Prospering Woman: A Complete Guide To Achieving The Abundant Life.* Warner, 0-931432-09-X $10.95. Written especially for women and jam packed with useful information. Ross is very effective in her presentation of issues which affect women from a psychological viewpoint. Valuable.

Shultz, Kennedy. *You Are The Power: A Guide To Greatness.* Hay House, 1-56170-074-6 $12.95. A lucid, witty and very useful book about using Science of Mind principles to enhance your life.

ABOUT THE AUTHOR

Jane Claypool was born in Texas, educated in California, and has also lived in New Jersey, Pennsylvania, Mexico, Massachusetts, and New York City. She now lives in Olivenhain, California, a suburb of San Diego.

Reverend Jane Claypool founded the Carlsbad Religious Science church in 1990. Before becoming an RSI minister, she had three other successful careers: teaching, writing and real estate marketing.

She is the author of seventy-one books for teenagers and was awarded Writer of the Year in 1981 by the Society of Children's Book Writers. Her pen names include Jane Claypool Miner and Veronica Ladd. The teen books have sold over two million copies and have been translated into seven languages. Her works have been published by Scholastic, Simon & Schuster, Franklin Watts and Avon, among others.

Claypool has also written hundreds of feature stories, scripts, and educational and business materials. Her client list includes *Reader's Digest, McGraw Hill*, and *The Writer Magazine*. She has worked on a newspaper and written newspaper columns.

Science of Mind Skills, her first metaphysical book, is being used in many New Thought churches as a supplemental class text. It is available in metaphysical bookstores or from Cornucopia Press. She is a frequent writer for *Creative Thought Magazine*.

Jane is a frequent speaker at conventions, workshops and organizations all over the nation. She also appears on national and local television and radio.

Between serving as pastor of a growing church, travelling nationally to promote the ideas in *Wise Women Don't Worry, Wise Women Don't sing the Blues* and working on new projects which include the *Wise Woman* newsletter, Wise Woman workbook and several new book ideas, Claypool is a busy woman.

"I love my life," Claypool says. "For the first time, I feel as if I'm fully functioning and using my talents in productive ways. As for energy - the energy is God's Unlimited Energy and it is always there. I look forward to every new adventure and that's a wonderful place to be."

When she isn't speaking, writing, travelling or signing books, Claypool is at home, "hanging out with my grandsons, reading - especially Victorian novels - and going to the movies or opera. It's a wonderful life."

FOR FURTHER STUDY

You can become a part of the Wise Woman network by writing to Cornucopia Press and asking to be placed on the Wise Woman mailing list.

Subscribe to the *Wise Woman Newsletter*. Published 6 times a year by Cornucopia Press. $18.00 per year.

Jane Claypool offers Wise Woman Facilitator training to a select few women who are interested in leading Wise Women groups in churches, community centers, college campuses, the workplace or their neighborhood. Ask how to obtain Wise Woman Facilitator training and certificate.

For information about Wise Women groups currently operating in your area, write or phone (619) 942-1628.

You can find metaphysical ideas and support for building a self-reliant life in Religious Science, Unity or other New Thought churches. There are also some excellent independent metaphysical churches in some areas of the nation. Look in the telephone book under Science of Mind, Religious Science, Unity, Divine Science or New Thought.

FOR MORE INFORMATION

Join the Wise Woman network:
_____ Put me on the Wise Woman mailing list.
_____ Start my subscription to the Wise Woman Newsletter.
       ($18.00 for six issues)
_____ Contact me about Wise Woman Facilitator Training.
_____ Give my name to local Wise Woman Facilitators.
_____ Contact me about speaking for my organization.

Read a book by Jane Claypool:
_____ Wise Women Don't Worry, Wise Women Don't Sing the
       Blues. $11.95
_____ Science of Mind Skills. $14.95

Listen to an audiotape by Jane Claypool:
_____ How to be a Wise Woman. $8.95
_____ Wise Woman Prosperity. $8.95
_____ Treatments and Affirmations from Science of Mind Skills.
       $13.95

Sales tax: Add 7% for items shipped to California.

Shipping: _____ First item: $2.00
                Each additional item: $.50
          _____ Priority Mail - $3.00 for 1-2 items

Please enclose payment with your order.

Name: _____

Address: _____

City, State, Zip: _____

Phone: _____

Complete and Mail To:
Cornucopia Press   This offer is subject to
PO Box 638   change without notice.
Encinitas, CA 92023
Or Call or Fax (619) 942-1628